TRUTH IN THE SON

Also by the same author

But This I *Can* Believe
The Search for the Real Jesus

TRUTH IN THE SON

David Winter

Is religious certainty a thing of the past?
Has God spoken to the human race?
If so, where?
And what has he said?

HODDER AND STOUGHTON
LONDON SYDNEY AUCKLAND TORONTO

British Library Cataloguing in Publication Data

Winter, David
   Truth in the Son.—(Hodder Christian paperbacks)
   1. Faith
   I. Title
  201   BT771.2

ISBN 0 340 39834 5

God
who gave to our forefathers
many different glimpses of the truth
has now
at the end of the present age
given us
the truth in the Son

Hebrews 1:1 *J. B. Phillips*

Contents

Preface   9

Introduction: Holy Communication   11

1   In the Beginning, God   17

2   An Infinite and Personal Creator?   31

3   Does God Intervene?   37

4   Has God 'Spoken'?   58

5   God As Communicator   66

6   The Bible – Inspired, or Inspiring?   75

7   Jesus of Nazareth: the Key?   85

Notes   109

Bibliography   112

Preface

Recent years have seen many attempts by writers, theologians and broadcasters to persuade us that religious certainty is a thing of the past. The Bible is unreliable and misleading. The Church has misunderstood its own creeds. The 'sea of faith' is on the ebb. In its most extreme form we have had the bizarre spectacle of ordained clergymen arguing that God – as an independently existing being – does not exist at all. Indeed, the Bible, creeds and even God himself are seen as part of the infancy of the human race, now to be abandoned so that we can move on to intellectual and spiritual maturity.

Not surprisingly, many Christians have been disturbed and dismayed by these views, well-publicised as they have been in the press, on television and radio. And undoubtedly others, who would not yet call themselves Christians, have begun to wonder whether it is worth looking for truth in a religion which is under such devastating attack from within the ranks of its own membership.

This book is addressed to both groups of people. It tries to show that the havoc has been caused not only by sceptical theologians but also by lazy Christians who have shirked the hard but rewarding task of thinking through a biblical faith in the modern world.

But it also tries to show that there is nothing inherently incredible in orthodox Christian belief – indeed, quite the contrary. The argument of this book is that there is no need for Christians to tremble for the faith, nor for seekers to look elsewhere, provided one simple premise is accepted: if there is purpose in life, only the intelligence that planned it can know what it is. If we cannot find it out, because it is literally beyond us, then we are thrown back on the only other reasonable proposition – it must be revealed to us.

INTRODUCTION: HOLY COMMUNICATION

I grew up in a remote rural village in Wales, without mains water, electricity or telephone. Water came from the village pump, light from hissing pressure oil-lamps, and warmth from coal and wood. Food was cooked in an oven built into the fireplace and the waste resulting from our consumption of it was disposed of in a little stone shed across the road, nicknamed *tŷ bach* in Welsh. On the sideboard in the living room stood a large wooden radio – which we called the wireless – with a wonderful fretwork face, from which there issued at daily intervals the world news, read from London, and not much else. The wet batteries could only be charged once a week, and when they were flat the radio was silent.

Today I sit in my lounge in a London suburb in a house which is almost totally dependent upon electricity to function properly, as we have found out to our cost in a number of infamous power-cuts. One of the things the electricity serves is the growing colony of electronic apparatus in the corner of the room – the hi-fi, the television set, the video and the teletext. Through these I am in contact with the world – or, more correctly, the world is in contact with me – day and night. At the touch of a switch I can have music, drama, news, information, comment and comedy whenever I want them. I can watch skiing in Yugoslavia, cricket in New Zealand, or a funeral in Moscow as they happen. I can dial a code and learn the latest movements of the world's markets, the day's temperature in far-off cities and the state of the roads in Scotland. Or I can turn a knob and hear voices from every corner of the world, an endless waterfall of words pouring out of the sky, arguing, pleading, cajoling, threatening, encouraging. In my own house I feel myself to be at the vortex of a great whirlpool of communication, a passive recipient of the world's ideas, opinions and news.

Of course all of these things are also now available in my childhood village. But the contrast, in the course of forty years or so, is staggering, and serves to illustrate the enormous change my generation has lived through. We have, moreover, survived to tell the tale. I find it amazing that octogenarians who were adults before even the days of wireless take television for granted, change channels at whim, and even complain that the programmes are not very good. We have all taken to the communication revolution with ease and alacrity, as though we had been waiting for it all along. Each new development – television, video, satellite – is taken in our stride, and quickly it becomes a familiar part of daily life. We may find other innovations difficult to cope with – supermarkets, perhaps, or motorways – but communication, even on the mass scale of the present day, seems to pose no threat.

The reason, surely, is that human beings are themselves communicators *par excellence*. Of all the creatures on this planet, none is so distinctively communicative as homo sapiens. We have an insatiable appetite for knowledge (even if it is only the local gossip) and an insatiable desire to pass it on to others (even if it is only a piece of sensational news). Our most distinctive feature, in the world of the animals, is not our ability to walk on our hind legs, or fashion artefacts with our hands, but to *speak*. It is man the verbaliser who has mastered his environment, ordered his society and enriched it with poetry, drama and song. Others may experience love, but only human beings can say 'I love you'. Others may be able to reason, but only mankind, with this priceless gift of language, can hold these ideas and concepts in the brain and then refine and develop them in recollection. It is not surprising that we have created a marvellous, if at times daunting and overwhelming, world of communication, for we are the great communicators, for whom the real horror words are 'isolation', 'loneliness' and 'silence', and the words of satisfaction, 'company', 'conversation' and 'involvement'.

It is rather sad that in this new world of communication the idea has begun to take root in some quarters that this is also the 'post-Christian' era. It seems to be assumed by some intellectuals that because the era of mass communication has coincided with a decline in the practice of religion, no one, in this brave new world of ideas and innovation, could possibly find room for the idea of a divine and personal intelligence who is at the heart of it.

I confess to finding this assumption both irritating and irrational. It seems to me that some theologians have been far too quick to abandon God. They have felt – on heaven knows what evidence – that modern people have outgrown the idea of an objectively real, infinite and personal God, and so some less exotic alternative must be found: a secular spirituality for a secular age. In earlier days – the 'times of our ignorance', perhaps – it was understandable that many people should hold superstitious and irrational ideas of a God 'out there' or 'up there', who created us, keeps us, hears us and, if we do what he requires of us, answers our prayers. But now (so the argument goes) mankind has come of age and is in the process of rejecting such outmoded concepts. The process, they concede, may be slow, but as knowledge and information spreads in the electronic renaissance, even ordinary people will inevitably turn away from these out-moded ideas to more acceptable and rational ones.

That is the argument which I hope to counter in this book. But at this point two things need to be said to clear the ground. The first is a matter of observation; the second an observation about the matter.

The first observation – irresistible to anyone like myself who has been reflecting and reporting on the religious scene for the last twenty-five years – is that there is no evidence at all that modern people are rejecting (no matter how slowly) the beliefs of traditional religion. Theologians may find that deplorable; they may even be right to do so. But not even theologians are allowed to ignore facts. And the fact is that traditional religion – conservative, even dogmatic religion – is stronger in almost every part of the world, and among all strata of society, than it was twenty-five or even fifty years ago.

In the world of Islam we have seen the resurgence of fundamentalism, and not only in Iran. A nascent movement to 'reform' Islam, to make it more acceptable to modern people by smoothing off its awkward edges and blunting some of its sharper demands, has been nipped in the bud, swamped by a floodtide of fanaticism. The Q'ran has been used as the sledge-hammer of this revival, in much the same way as the new Christian fundamentalism – mainly in the United States, but increasingly elsewhere, too – uses the Bible.

That new fundamentalism is also a growing force. Theologians delude themselves if they think this is simply a movement of the psychologically deprived and the theologically illiterate. It is, much more accurately, a reaction against a form of Christianity that promised a lot and delivered little – the bloodless, 'liberal' Christianity of the recent past.

That reaction also shows itself in many other ways – the new confidence of the Roman Catholic Church under its present traditional leadership; the shift in the main Protestant Churches towards a more conservative theology; the growth in church membership in the United States and of the house church movement in Britain; the rise in sales of the Bible in a score of versions, and the astonishing revival of evangelical Christianity in the universities of the Western world. In the face of all this, it would be no exaggeration to say that those who claim the modern world has 'taken leave of God' (in Don Cupitt's phrase) have themselves taken leave of the facts.

At the same time, the growth of several doctrinaire sects – movements like the Mormons and Jehovah's Witnesses, whose growth rate even in Western countries is remarkable – and the fascination, not to say obsession of millions of people with the irrational appeal of astrology, contradict the argument that modern man has moved out of the era of superstition into the post-religious age. If anything, the evidence suggests that the Graeco-Roman world of the time of Christ was less superstitious than ours today. It is true that they too believed in astrology, but I think they would have found it hard to credit a television astrologer claiming to give mass predictions for millions of people at a time, or newspaper predictions of quite staggering banality, totally lacking in the sophistication of a Delphic oracle.

I am not saying, of course, that Christianity is to be equated with astrology, the sects or even its own fanatical fundamentalist fringes. Indeed, I do not believe that it is any less 'rational' than the secular alternatives on offer. But it does require the humility to concede that the universe may be such that unaided human intelligence, no matter how technologically ingenious, simply cannot comprehend it. That is what has always created the greatest problem for the arrogant intellectual.

The second observation – of the other kind, a comment on the evidence – is that it is not at all surprising that an era of communication should coincide with an era of faith in God. I have tried, in a brief sketch, to show the extent to which human beings are communicators – not as an optional extra, but as an integral part of their humanity. Is it surprising, then, that they should look for a God who communicates?

The Bible says that men and women are made 'in the image of God'. They reflect something of his nature. God creates; and we, in our little way, also create. God loves; and we, through whatever mists of malice and misunderstanding, also love. God speaks, God communicates; and we, at every level from local gossip to intercontinental satellite, from the drama of Shakespeare to the nervous explanations of a pair of lovers, communicate.

But we should observe the order. Our love of creating things – art, furniture, hair-styles – is a reflection of a creator God. Our love is a reflection of a loving God. And our communication, even in all its modern diversity, is a reflection of a God who speaks.

God communicates with us. That, for me, is the single most important thing one can know about the world we live in. Deafened by call-signs and tone and bleeps and the endless prattle of the air-waves, it is possible that the people of the great age of communication may fail to hear the voice of the Great Communicator. Sadly, that is both more likely and more serious than the possibility that those same people may drift into a 'post-Christian' era.

God exists, and God has spoken. That, at any rate, is the argument of this book. It may be that when you get to the last page you will feel that the case has not been proven, and even, perhaps, that the secular theologians are right, and we must look for a spiritual reality that does not require an objectively real, infinite and personal God, or listen for his voice.

I believe that if God does exist then he must have spoken. In a creation alive with communication it would seem to me above everything else incredible if the God who made and sustains it has not communicated with us. Whatever one might expect of the God who made people like us, it is not *silence*.

1 IN THE BEGINNING, GOD

The Bible does not argue for the existence of God. Indeed, from its very first sentence it takes his existence for granted: 'In the beginning God created the heavens and the earth' (Genesis 1:1). The succeeding books of the Old Testament contain no doctrine of God, and offer no organised or coherent information about his nature. What they do give us is a picture of his activity in the created world, and especially in humankind.

It is perhaps for this reason that some strange ideas of God have always been popularly believed. It is widely assumed, for instance, that Christians believe the world was created and is sustained by a male person inhabiting some remote realm of outer space. It is also supposed that this Person is responsible in a direct cause-and-effect way for every occurrence on this planet, from missed trains to blighted crops, and that he has his own way of rewarding the good and making the evil-doer suffer.

Others, no doubt appalled at the moral problems created by such notions, have moved to the opposite extreme. They see God as abstract substance, almighty impersonal energy or the personification of some such concept as love, truth or beauty. In each case, he is thereby removed from involvement with human beings in any personal way, and cannot be held directly responsible for the various immoralities and injustices which manifestly flourish in the universe he has created.

The problem is that all of these ideas *can* be found in the biblical picture of God. Indeed, rather worse ones can be:

that God is the tribal deity of Israel, quite content that other races shall be put to the sword if only his chosen people may flourish; or that he is a party to various political or military stratagems of an unsavoury nature, carried out at his behest or with his connivance.

Yet although these ideas are in the Bible, they do not add up to the biblical picture of God. To establish that, we must work to certain ground-rules. Firstly, the picture must be seen *whole*: only confusion will ensue if we isolate certain parts and magnify them, or ignore other parts which we find unattractive.

Then, we must accept that if God is God we can *only* know of him by his own self-revelation: 'Can *you* fathom the mysteries of God?' asked Zophar of Job (Job 11:7). If he is to be known at all, the Creator must reveal himself to his creatures. He must communicate with us before we can in any realistic way communicate with him. This communication can take many different forms, but if God is almighty and all-knowing (and what sort of a 'god' would he be if he were not?) we are dependent upon him to let us know what he is like. This means that what he is perceived to have done and said in human history is the only evidence we have of him – though that includes, of course, our own experiences of him.

Thirdly, and following on from that, we shall expect the biblical picture of God to become clearer with the passage of time. We shall not be surprised to discover that the ideas of God expressed by our remote forefathers in the era of prehistory are imperfect and at times crude. If the revelation of God is woven into the texture of human history, it must be a progressive thing, as history is. So the Bible's picture of God becomes clearer as its story unfolds.

In the Bible, after the majestic vision of creation, we are for long stretches given the picture of God as little more than a tribal deity, superior to, but not in essence different from the gods of other peoples. Even here there are hints of greater things, but as we move on through the history of

Israel, and especially into the books of the great prophets, a richer picture emerges. Here God is a universal moral arbiter, a righteous, patient, sublime spiritual being, high and lifted up, above all things holy. And then, in the New Testament, we have another dimension added, with the picture of God as Father, loving and caring for the whole world. The biblical picture must be seen whole, as I have said, but the end is greater than the beginning and there is nothing strange about the fact that man's idea of God has grown from humble and primitive origins to the magnificent vision of God as the Father of Jesus.

This is an important principle, but often overlooked. Christians are worried by ideas about God found in parts of the Old Testament, and find them hard to reconcile with New Testament ideas. What they are in fact doing is to demand that the human race should from the first have had access to complete and perfect knowledge about God. Yet no one would expect to find in ancient writings a concept of, say, number as sophisticated as that of modern mathematics. This hardly discredits the principle of number any more than primitive ideas of God discredit the biblical principle of divinity. Mathematics – that is, the principle of number – has never changed. Neither has God. But, in both cases, as time has passed we have discovered more and more about the subject, the picture has become clearer, the principle has become better known. And that fact is still true even if one asserts, as Christians do, that it is God who reveals himself in history, rather than people who discover him in it.

What kind of a 'God'?

The difficulty about the word 'God' is that it can mean pretty well whatever you want it to. Not only that, but it has to cover ideas of a divine being as varied as the gods of Greece and Rome, on the one extreme, and the 'God' of Buddhism on the other: from human beings playing at divinity to human beings finding some concept of divinity within them. And in the midst of this complicated supermarket of supreme beings stands the God of the Bible – the God of Christians and Jews, 'Yahweh' (to give him his name) or 'Almighty God' (to give him his occupation).

So when modern critics argue against the existence of God, it is necessary to enquire what kind of a god they have in mind. Certainly a careful critic will need to spend a great deal of time defining the nature of the God he is seeking to disprove, or he may be in danger of convincing his readers only that a god no one believes in has no objective existence. That is hardly the stuff of Sunday paper headlines.

However, there have been scholars willing to shoulder the burden and try. One of the best-known, Don Cupitt, has argued, in a book called *Taking Leave of God*, that we should part company with the thought of an objective God, as something belonging to a bygone age. He then argues for a 'God' within us, 'internalised', apparent only in terms of 'religious values', and having no authority or objective reality.

Writers like Cupitt start from the premise that modern man has outgrown the idea of God. Having rejected the Aristotelian or medieval idea of a Divine Being who sets things in motion, or controls them from his place in heaven above, they seem to assume that this is also the biblical view of God. So he, too, is dismissed as irrelevant to our modern understanding of the world we live in.

Some scientists have arrived at much the same conclusion, but from very different arguments. For them, God is no longer 'necessary' as an explanation for existence, or as lending meaning or purpose to it. Not all of them are atheists, by any means, but they do not see a role for God in the physical universe. A BBC television programme[1] brought to the general public in Britain the ideas of a young American professor of physics, Alan Guth, whose new 'Inflationary

Theory' of creation was said to have offered an answer to one of the deepest questions of all: 'Where does the universe come from?'

Guth suggests that after the initial 'Big Bang' the universe went through an extraordinary explosive expansion. In a flicker of time, according to this theory, all the matter that we see in the universe today was produced, as energy was siphoned from the gravitational field. The theory has been dubbed the 'Free Lunch Account', because it produces matter apparently out of nothing.

In fact, it is not out of nothing, for hiding in a corner of this fascinating theory is the rather disarming concession that it is necessary to start with 'a few kilogrammes' of matter. Where, we may ask, did those 'few kilogrammes' come from? Guth has a theory there too. It depends on gravity and Quantum mechanics and suggests that the geometry of the universe can 'randomly change from a state of absolute nothingness to a state of a very small universe which contains those few initial kilogrammes of matter'. This 'seed' universe then violently explodes, growing by the process of inflation to produce the universe that we see. By this theory, the laws of physics started with absolutely nothing and created our universe out of the void.

But now we are starting with something else, the 'laws of physics'. Where did *they* come from? John Polkinghorne, formerly professor of Mathematical Physics at Cambridge University, now an Anglican priest, argues that they originate in the will of God. Peter Atkins, of the Department of Physical Chemistry at Oxford University, and an atheist, believes that their existence is a logical necessity. As they are the only possible set of laws that could be in any universe, if the universe exists, so must they!

To the layman, all that seems clear from these arguments is that there is no irresistible scientific reason why one should abandon belief in God as creator. The concept is not fantastic, irrelevant, irrational or archaic. Equally well-informed people take opposite sides in the argument, often depending on preconceptions about the evidence. The question that really haunts the whole discussion is not so much 'Is there a God?' as 'What do we mean by "God"?'

Many of the theological sceptics and most of the scientific sceptics seem to me to have a common idea of the God who does not exist. He is the God of Western folk culture. He is the God of miracles, the God who intervenes, the God who makes and maintains rule and order in the universe, and exists as a personal Being somewhere within it. He is the God who is responsible for every occurrence on this planet, from drought in Ethiopia to floods in Bangladesh, from a missed bus to a fatal heart attack. *But he is not the God of the Bible*.

Now that assertion may surprise some people. Surely the eminent theologians who write these books which demand that 'our image of God must go' are familiar with the God of the Bible? Surely it *is* the God of the Bible that they are rejecting?

My suspicion is that many of them are rather more familiar with German theology and philosophy than they are with the Old and New Testaments. Certainly they make assumptions about what they call the 'traditional' view of God which seem to betray a less than profound grasp of what the Bible actually says about him. Sometimes they seem to be erecting a paper god in order to show how flimsy and useless he is. Sometimes they too readily accept the 'God' of popular hymnology or superstitious devotion as though that were the God of the Bible, and have little difficulty in ridiculing and rejecting him.

Of course many Christian believers still have an inadequate – indeed, indefensible – notion of God. That is all but inevitable when folk religion and popular myth have had nearly twenty centuries in which to distort the Christian doctrine of God. Ideas get handed on from generation to generation. Phrases enter the language, enjoying a status equivalent to holy writ: 'God helps those who help themselves' . . . 'Why has God done this to me?' . . . 'Please God he'll recover' . . . 'Thank God it was near a phone-box' . . .

'You are nearer God's heart in a garden than anywhere else on earth.'

Even people who know that these are not biblical concepts are influenced by the ideas behind them: that God rewards the good and punishes the evil, that God is responsible for pain and suffering, that recovery from ill-health, or death, are his direct responsibility, that he manipulates motor-cars, punctures and even the availability of the breakdown van, and that he prefers gardens, hills and streams to tower-blocks, tenements and slums.

There is some truth in some of those ideas, of course. Indeed, it could be argued that they are nothing worse than deviant understandings of perfectly orthodox beliefs about God. But it is that 'deviant understanding' that has laid people open to the arguments of the sceptics. For instance, it is not part of the biblical revelation of God that he is 'out there', occupying some unknown corner of the universe. But if people read an article in which a distinguished theologian argues that God is not 'out there', and in fact does not occupy *any* place at all in the universe, they feel threatened and react indignantly. Equally, it is not part of the biblical revelation that God is male, in the sexual or gender sense. How can he be, when he is 'Spirit' – 'without body, parts or passions', as the Thirty-Nine Articles put it? Yet many Christians are deeply disturbed to be told that God is not male, as though that were to deny his personality.

The fact that many believers have an inadequate view of God does not excuse writers who have taken the popular misconceptions and used them to pour scorn on the biblical view of God. If we are to find a God 'acceptable' to modern thought the first step is surely to correct popular misunder-standings, rather than to imply that they reflect the biblical understanding of God and must be abandoned.

The God of the Bible

The God of the Bible is, as we have seen, progressively revealed. But right from the start he is seen as the Creator, the originator of all that exists:

In the beginning God created the heavens and the earth.

It is important to establish what this claim means. It does not necessarily mean, for example, that God individually fashioned each creature or each species, nor that he made the stars and planets out of nothing. He may have done, but no such claim is made by the writer of Genesis. What he does assert, and it is a common theme of the Bible, is that all that exists emanates from God. He is the Creator, rather than the Maker. A maker takes what already exists – wood, glue, pins – and fashions from it something new – a chair, perhaps. But a creator, like a musical composer, takes an idea, a concept in his or her own mind, and turns it into something audible, visible or tangible.

This is an important distinction, because it means that God is not regarded principally as the 'first cause' so much as the architect and planner of the universe. Many of the scientific and pseudo-scientific arguments against the existence of God relate to the origins of matter. They assert that there is no evidence for the creation of matter out of nothing, and that it is in any case intrinsically irrational to have a non-material being, 'spirit', as the origin or source of matter.

I am not convinced that it *is* irrational, or that this argument makes due allowance for the potential relationship of the spiritual to the material, which we shall be exploring later. But even if we take it at face value, to assert that God is the Creator of all that is is to say much more than that he is merely the origin or source of matter. It is to say that he is the conscious mind behind the whole process.

In one sense, the first living cell to come into being

contained within itself the 'plan' for all that followed. All that has developed in the as yet uncharted course from simple cells to life in all its present varied forms and ultimately in self-conscious human life has followed a coding. That coding locked into the first living cells the potential which we see realised over the vast ages of our planet's history. This is the very opposite of blind chance. It is the trade mark of the intelligence that transcends matter, and its existence is far more important than arguments about its origin. What use would a few molecules of matter be without an overriding plan?

It is the Christian case, the biblical case, that God is the author of that 'plan', the intelligence that has shaped creation. The Old Testament psalmist put it in vivid poetic language:

> For you created my inmost being;
> you knit me together in my mother's womb.
> I praise you because I am fearfully and
>   wonderfully made;
> your works are wonderful,
> I know that full well.
> My frame was not hidden from you
> when I was made in the secret place.
> When I was woven together in the
>   depths of the earth,
> your eyes saw my unformed body.
> All the days ordained for me
> were written in your book
> before one of them came to be.[2]

Of course people are free to argue that there is no plan, no purpose in creation, that it is the product of blind chance. But it is a position that is becoming harder and harder to sustain, as we shall see.

If there *is* a plan, then it must (so far as we can possibly conceive) be the product of mind, and mind involves (again,

so far as we can possibly conceive) personality. When the
Bible says that God is the Creator, it is an assertion about
mind rather than matter, as the awesome language of the
opening passage of Genesis underlines. The key verbs of
God's activity are intellectual actions: God willed, God
spoke, God saw.

> In the beginning God created the heavens and the earth.
> Now the earth was formless and empty, darkness was over
> the surface of the deep, and the Spirit of God was hovering
> over the waters.
>
> And *God said*, 'Let there be light,' and there was light.
> *God saw* that the light was good, and he separated the light
> from the darkness. *God called* the light day and the
> darkness he called night. And there was evening and there
> was morning – the first day.
>
> And *God said*, 'Let there be an expanse between the
> waters to separate water from water.' So God made the
> expanse and separated the water under the expanse from
> the water above it. And it was so. *God called* the expanse
> sky. And there was evening, and there was morning – the
> second day.
>
> And *God said*, 'Let the water under the sky be gathered
> to one place, and let dry ground appear.' And it was so.
> *God called* the dry ground land and the gathered waters he
> called 'seas'. And *God saw* that it was good.
>
> Then *God said*, 'Let the land produce vegetation: seed-
> bearing plants and trees on the land that bear fruit with
> seed in it, according to their various kinds.' And it was so.
> The land produced vegetation: plants bearing seed accord-
> ing to their kinds and trees bearing fruit with seed in it
> according to their kinds. And *God saw* that it was good.
> And there was evening, and there was morning – the third
> day.[3]

Now all of this is not just mental gymnastics. It actually
matters that we understand what we mean when we say that

God is the 'creator', because most of those who argue against 'creation' do so, it seems to me, on a misunderstanding of the Bible's claims. They allege that Christians believe that God conjured up matter out of nowhere and nothing, and that by a series of specific actions he then fashioned out of that matter the universe, this planet, plant and animal life and human-kind. Various scientific and philosophical arguments are then applied to this thesis to demonstrate that it is logically untenable.

There are two things to say about this. The first is that that is not (except in the crudest caricature) the biblical case for divine creation. The second is that, even in that crude form, it is neither illogical nor untenable.

To take the second first, there is a great danger for all of us – believers and unbelievers – of overstating our case. The truth is that, despite all our scientific advances, we know precious little, if anything, about the origin of matter. We still have to say, like the medieval philosophers, that there are only two possibilities. Either things have always been like this (that is, matter has always existed), or there was a first cause utterly unlike anything that has ever happened since – unlike, because everything we know has come from some-thing that preceded it, is 'contingent', in the old jargon, and the 'first cause' cannot have been contingent because if it had been it would not have been the first.

No amount of sophisticated argument can really get beyond these two theses. However far back we trace matter and to whatever primitive forms, either it had an origin, a beginning, or matter has always existed. The latter looks the less tenable position – though the arguments go back and forwards like a tennis rally – which leaves us with the fascinating question, 'What is the origin of matter?' No matter how dedicated we are to any theory of origins or evolution, that question lies behind it. The out-and-out creationist, who says that God brought matter into being by a deliberate act of his will, is not proposing something that is illogical or untenable. It may be unpalatable to some people, but it is, so far as I can see, incapable of being disproved and, like all good hypotheses, it explains the known facts without contradicting itself.

However, that is not the biblical case for creation, or, at any rate, it does not do it full justice. The Bible's picture of creation is far more sophisticated than some of its own keennest protagonists seem to realise, or some of its most articulate opponents are prepared to allow.

The heart of the biblical case is something I have already referred to: creation is seen as a mental rather than physical activity. Of course it had physical *results* – these are described in the opening chapters of Genesis in phrases of simple and memorable beauty – but the creative activity of God is described in the Bible entirely in intellectual terms. This theme is a common one all through the Bible – that God is the mind, the purpose, the architect of all that is, that it exists by his design and to fulfil his will:

> The heavens are yours, and yours also the earth;
> you founded the world and all that is in it.
> You created the north and the south;
> Tabor and Hermon sing for joy at your name.[4]

> I am the LORD, and there is no other.
> I form the light and create darkness,
> I bring prosperity and create disaster;
> I, the LORD, do all these things.[5]

> You are worthy, our Lord and God,
> to receive glory and honour and power,
> for you created all things,
> and by your will they were created
> and have their being.[6]

Now, it may reasonably be objected that plans and designs have to be carried out, and that to say God is the architect is not to deny that he is also the builder. That is true, at one level. The universe is not, in Judaeo-Christian thought, a 'dream in the mind of God'. It is a physical reality, it actually exists.

But the biblical priority is clear, it seems to me. The important thing is the divine will. How that will brought about the physical world is a question of mechanics which we do not, and may never, understand. But the evidence for the presence in the created world of order and design is before our eyes or under our microscopes, and most scientists are aware of it. John Polkinghorne has put it like this: 'You could say that the most remarkable thing about science is that it is possible at all, that the world is orderly and our minds are capable of perceiving the order.' For him, the beauty revealed in the structure of the world was 'like a rehabilitation of the argument from design'.[7]

It is true that we cannot at present see how the concept of a divine mind shaping the universe translates itself into the universe of order and design which we live in and observe, but that does not in any important way argue against its existence.

It is fascinating that the opening words of the Old Testament and the opening words of the Fourth Gospel in the New Testament offer 'God' and 'Word' as the description of that which was there 'in the beginning':

In the beginning, God . . .
In the beginning was the Word . . .

John pursues the argument in an intriguing way:

In the beginning was the Word, and the Word was with God, and the Word was God. He was with God in the beginning.
   Through him all things were made; without him nothing was made that has been made. In him was life, and that life was the light of men. The light shines in the darkness, but the darkness has not understood (or, overcome) it.[8]

The parallel with the opening of Genesis is plain:

> In the beginning God created the heavens and the earth. Now the earth was formless and empty, darkness was over the surface of the deep, and the Spirit of God was hovering over the waters.
>
> And God said, 'Let there be light', and there was light . . .[9]

The themes are identical: God, darkness and the coming of light. The difference is in the identification of the role of the 'Word' – *logos*, in Greek.

There is, of course, a word, or words, in Genesis, too: 'Let there be light.' God *speaks* and something happens. This is no ordinary word, because it creates, it causes, it brings something into being.

But so does the Word in the Fourth Gospel. The *logos* – Jesus – is not just a concept, a philosophy or an idea. The Word is no ordinary word. He, too, creates, causes, brings something – no, *everything* – into being: 'Without him nothing was made that has been made.' The absolute heart of the biblical idea of creation is 'the Word': the plan, purpose and expression of God. God spoke, God expressed himself, in the creation. Just as (John argues) Jesus was God in human form, so the creation is a material expression of God. It is not magic, but divine will. The world we see and the life we live are part of a plan devised and carried out by God.

2 AN INFINITE AND PERSONAL CREATOR?

We are just emerging from a period in history – brief, in comparison with the ages of human existence, but dominant because it is so recent – in which most educated people were afraid to speak of such a 'plan' of creation or of a divine intelligence shaping the creative process. Darwin's *Origin of Species* provided an apparently rational explanation, which seemed to enable mankind to cast off once and for all the distasteful idea of a divine Being who created and sustains the universe (and, one might add, makes moral demands of his creatures). The principle of the survival of the fittest suited the temper of the time; indeed, it is the very dynamo of Imperialism. Chance mutations seemed a satisfactory explanation for all the living forms we see around us – given enough time, and the operation of the process of natural selection. For more than a century the Theory of Evolution, carried further than Darwin probably intended, has dominated the natural sciences and emasculated biblical theology. There is no God but chance; there is no divine will, simply natural selection.

But today the whole edifice is collapsing. Few people would argue that evolution is not a fact of biological and species development, but as an explanation for the presence of life on earth in all its varied forms, and especially for the existence of the human race, it is now widely regarded as totally inadequate.

In a lecture broadcast on Radio 3, which proposed ideas set

out in a subsequent book[1], Professor Fred Hoyle argued the
fundamental irrationality of those who see evolution as an
explanation for the origin and development of biological
forms. There has not been enough *time*, he argues. There is
no evidence to support the theory that mutations lead to
improvements: quite the contrary – though some biologists
sharply disagree with him over this. And, he says, the odds
against the particular chain of proteins being present in the
order they need to be to bring about life in every single one of
its manifestations are, in his own words, 'super-
astronomical'. There is no doubt, he asserts, that the origin
of biological forms lies *outside* them, rather than within them.

Hoyle's argument is, at heart, mathematical. For him, the
Achilles heel of evolution as an explanation is its extreme
unlikeliness. Indeed, he goes further and suggests it is so
fantastically improbable that no rational person would support it as an explanation, if any viable alternative were
offered.

Hoyle then offers three alternatives. The first is that life
originated not on the surface of our planet but elsewhere in
our universe. He concedes that this only pushes the problem
one stage back – it still does not explain how life began. But
it has for him one other and crucial advantage: it extends the
mathematical possibilities. Given enough time and enough
options, evolution might make sense. The universe offers
more time and infinitely more options. Hence Hoyle's
views – rejected, it must be said, by many of his scientific
colleagues – about the presence of micro-organisms in inter-
stellar space.

The second view Hoyle offers – and it is complementary
to rather than a contradiction of the first – is that the whole
process of life has been planned and is being controlled by a
creative intelligence. He asserts that all the evidence sup-
ports this; it is fear of religion (and fear of being thought
naïve) that prevents scientists from following the logic of
their own observations. They are worried by the way everything in the universe fits just right: the size of basic atomic

particles, the proportion of carbon and oxygen. And they cannot explain the apparently sudden and random leaps forward in the chain of evolution. Yet they are reluctant to draw what he sees as the obvious conclusion: that an overarching intelligence is behind the whole process. It was that intelligence which devised the 'coding' that has predetermined the development of life from primitive cells to articulate and self-aware human beings.

This 'intelligence' or 'creator' is, in this theory, *within* the created universe, not outside it. That means, of course, that it is part of what it has brought into being – a problem he recognises but does not answer.

His third possibility answers it very well: that the universe is the work of such a creative being as the Judaeo-Christian God, intervening as he did with Moses through the burning bush. Hoyle is not ready to take the step of settling for this particular option, though he raises no serious intellectual arguments against it. He seems suspicious of the 'religious view' (as he calls it) which believes that the universe was created to make it right for life in all its subsequent forms. He prefers to see a continuous process of conscious and intelligent adjustment and improvement.

Such a possibility is in fact also hinted at in the Bible, where God is not seen simply as a remote Creator who set the process in motion and now watches it fulfilling some arbitrary plan. This is an eighteenth century idea, rather than a biblical one. Often the Bible shows us God as *involved* in the life of his world, sustaining and controlling it, intimately and even affectionately present in the very processes of biology by which life is renewed.

> For you created my inmost being;
> you knit me together in my mother's womb.[2]

Whatever we make of Hoyle's arguments, he has, at any rate, reintroduced the whole idea of *evidence* into the argument between evolution and creation. He feels that there has been an unhelpful pact between scientists and theologians to exclude scientific evidence from the debate about God. Both 'sides', it must be confessed, are to be found asserting that God can neither be proved nor disproved by science. Hoyle thinks it is at any rate possible that he (or it) *could* be.

That would interest Christians, of course, but scientific evidence which appeared to prove the presence of a creative intelligence at work in our universe would not clinch the case for belief in the Judaeo-Christian God, even if it did make atheism in its traditional forms totally untenable. The God of the Bible possesses a creative intelligence, true; but he is much more than that, and it is the 'much more' that is important in the Christian view of existence.

Firstly, the God of the Bible is not part of what he has brought into being. God would not cease to exist if the universe ceased to exist, just as he did not come into being when matter came into being. Although that idea – of the infinite nature of God – is difficult (indeed, in the literal sense of the word, incomprehensible), it does not carry the built-in contradictions and limitations of Hoyle's 'second' thesis, that the creative intelligence is within our universe and hence, presumably, part of it. Hoyle himself talks of life being 'deliberately started'. Surely, then, the 'starter' – whoever or whatever it is – must have existed before the plan was put into action? To put it crudely, if you are going to have a god, you might as well have a proper one.

Secondly, the God of the Bible is not an impersonal intelligence. It is easy, of course, to try to score cheap debating points here. We cannot conceive of creative intelligence apart from personality, but that does not mean that the idea is inherently impossible. However, personality is certainly the highest product of life that we can conceive, and it seems unlikely, to say the least, that the intelligence that planned it and brought it into being should be less than personal. That is not, of course, to say it is bodily – a sort of superhuman in the sky. But it is to say that creative intelligence and personality do seem to have a universal link, and when Christians say that God is personal they are, in part at least, recognising it at the highest imaginable level.

The third thing which takes the Christian view of God beyond the notion of merely a super-intelligence is its belief that God is good. He is not morally neutral; he is not evil; he is positively, totally and innately good.

It is true that a superficial assessment of the world he has made might not lead to that conclusion. How could a good Creator have planned an environment of such pervasive misery? The majority of human kind throughout recorded history have passed their days in fear, deprivation, exploitation and pain. Is this the handiwork of a Person who is 'positively, totally and innately good'?

Yet it must be said that the majority of human beings have also experienced joys of an intense and satisfying goodness: love, music, art, friendship, parenthood – can these be by-products of a creative process planned by an evil, or morally indifferent, intelligence? The presence of these two elements in human experience has puzzled the human race since the dawn of history. No better explanation has yet been offered than the Christian doctrine of the 'Fall' – that mankind was created good but, by the exercise of a moral freedom given it by God, chose to do evil. It may sound like no more than a device intended to get God off a particularly awkward moral hook, but as a description of the facts as we see them no one has yet improved on it. This looks like a world created by a good God – a world of beauty, truth and love – and yet tragically marred by the hatred, greed and injustice of mankind. The Fall may seem a crude explanation, but at least it fits. God is good, the earth is fair: 'man alone is vile' – not always, and not irreversibly, but deeply flawed.

The God of the Bible is infinite, personal and good. That is a long way on from the idea of a creative intelligence which is itself contained within the universe. It is also a long way on from the internalised 'God' of those modern theologians who regard notions of an 'objectively real' God as belonging to a bygone age. It is slightly ironic that at the moment when some secular scientists are rediscovering the intellectual attractiveness of the idea of an objectively real 'God' planning and directing life, some Christian theologians are urging us to abandon it!

As so often in the past, intellectual fashions come and go but the God of the Bible survives them all. There is a peculiar resilience in this picture of an infinite, personal and good Creator. It has been distorted by Christians, ridiculed by humanists, ignored by secularists and challenged by various scientific and philosophical fashions. But it continually emerges unscathed, and indeed often enhanced by its ability to meet new challenges and throw light on new problems. Far from being an intellectual embarrassment, the biblical doctrine of God will undoubtedly emerge once again in the closing decades of this century as the strongest plank in the Church's platform. History will wonder why for more than a century Christians lost their nerve and all but abandoned it. Opponents and sympathetic doubters will be compelled to see its intellectual integrity and unity.

The idea of an objectively real, infinite, personal and good God as the Creator of the universe and of life gives meaning and dignity to our existence. That would not in itself be a sufficient reason for believing it if it were not true. But if it is, it is, quite simply, the most important thing in the world to know.

3 DOES GOD INTERVENE?

The popular – some would say, primitive – view of God is that he is responsible, in a direct cause-and-effect way, for everything that happens. So the farmer prays to him for rain, the shipwrecked sailor for rescue, the pregnant woman for a safe delivery, the warrior-king for success in battle. At a different level, there are devoutly religious people who believe that God orders such details of their personal lives as the purchase of a new coat, the choice of a new home or even the availability of a parking meter. At a third, and more sophisticated level, most Christians would subscribe to the view that God sometimes 'intervenes' miraculously in human affairs, to bring people to faith in Jesus, to deliver the Church from destruction or to heal the incurably ill. They would regard it as unthinkable to doubt that God has the right, the power and the will to do what he wishes in the world he has created.

But there are theologians today who are prepared to think the unthinkable, in this as in other areas. For them, there is a certain attraction in the idea of a 'weak' or 'limited' God, who cannot and does not intervene to put things right, but only suffers alongside his creatures. For them, the cross of Jesus is the supreme symbol of divinity. They speak of a 'suffering' God, and see his power, in the words of St Paul, as 'made perfect in weakness' (2 Corinthians 12:9).

These theologians are aware of the danger of God being regarded like the *deus ex machina* of Greek drama, who stepped on to the stage when things were totally out of hand and sorted everything out. They realise that quite a lot of popular Christianity has perpetuated some such idea of God.

At heart, they do not like the notion of God as someone who 'steps in' or is 'called in' to rescue lost causes, whether they concern seamen in life-rafts or patients dying of cancer. God is present, everywhere and all the time, within his creation. He does not have to be 'called in', because he is there already. His role is not to intervene in, but to identify with human sorrows, anxieties and suffering. In other words, they reject the very idea of God as a miraculous intervenor in human affairs.

In essence, this is no new argument. Theologians have argued ever since the early days of the Christian Church about the extent to which God is *above* or *within* his creation: transcendent or immanent. Some Christians have always emphasised God's transcendence – that he is the 'totally other', the One who 'sits upon the throne of the universe', the all-seeing, all-knowing, all-powerful Creator God. Others have emphasised his immanence – that he is the God who is the Father of Jesus, the God who identified with the people of Israel ('in all their distress he too was distressed') who is 'closer . . . than breathing, and nearer than hands and feet', as Tennyson put it. The two views have never been regarded as irreconcilable, and the different emphases have generally balanced each other over church history so well that the classic doctrine of God as *both* transcendent *and* immanent has not been threatened.

But now this doctrine is under attack. If God *cannot* intervene in human affairs, if he *never* does more than identify with our problems, if he *will not* answer a call to act on our behalf, then he is not the God of the Bible. Transcendence has gone, and so has any notion of God as the ruler of the universe. Is that, however, what is being alleged? It certainly sounds like it, but there are two important provisos which can put a rather different interpretation on the argument.

The first is whether this limitation on God as intervenor arises simply by his own will, or because it is part of his very nature. To put it simply, is it that God *cannot* intervene, because he does not have the ability to do so, or is it that God has, by his own will, *decided* not to intervene? If God cannot act, cannot, for instance, overrule the laws of nature or alter in any way the course of history – either in vast, global issues or in the minute particulars of a person's life – then he is not transcendent. Indeed, it is hard to see how he is God at all, in any normal meaning of the word. 'Transcendent', after all, means 'above everything', which presumably must mean above what he has himself made.

On the other hand, if God has simply decided, by his own will, not to intervene, although he has the power to do so, then the notion of transcendence is preserved, though it would seem to be evacuated of any practical meaning. This notion sees God as *voluntarily* excluding himself from interfering in the course of events, beyond identifying himself with the human condition and struggling within us. He helps us, in other words, within ourselves, not by altering our circumstances.

The other proviso concerns the duration of this limitation on God's power to act. There is obviously a very great difference between saying that God (either voluntarily, or by his nature) cannot ever intervene in history, and saying that God is refraining (or is restrained) from doing so for a specific reason and for a specific period of time. In this view, the incarnation is crucial. God identified with us in Jesus, and initiated a period of human history in which his activity in the world would be limited to the continuing effect of that incarnation. Jesus, present on this planet for thirty-three years, and 'present' through his followers ever since, is at work on God's behalf in his world – not by manipulating the set pieces of history, but by the influence of the 'body of Christ', the Church. The biblical pictures of this are the yeast, slowly spreading through the dough and transforming it, and the salt, pervasive and highly effective in countering corruption and decay.

These two provisos – that God's limitation is voluntary and temporary – are important, but they do not seem to me to meet the requirements of the full biblical view of God. They are not argued from biblical evidence, but from observation of the world. They do not start from what God has revealed about himself, but from our human perception of what he is like. God has not told us that he has limited his own power to intervene, either permanently or temporarily. The undeniable fact that he identified with our suffering and weakness in Jesus tells us something important about God which it would have been hard to discover from the Old Testament, but it does not follow that all the other attributes of God revealed before the coming of Jesus are thereby abrogated. The Cross tells us that God's power is perfected in weakness, true. But does not the resurrection which immediately followed it tell us that God still 'intervenes'? Is it not set out in the New Testament as the *supreme* example of God's power? It is a strange theology that talks of the cross as though the resurrection had never happened (and that is true however or in whatever way one chooses to understand the resurrection).

Indeed, if the Cross is the paradigm of God's weakness, for the apostles the resurrection was the paradigm of his power: '*By his power* God raised the Lord from the dead' (I Corinthians 6:14). The two events emphasise yet again the complementarity of the two attributes of God, his immanence and his transcendence. The derelict, broken figure on the Cross tells me that God is with me; the risen Lord – 'the radiance of God's glory' (Hebrews 1:3) – tells me that God still reigns in his universe. It may hurt modern susceptibilities to say so, but for Christians the belief that God is ultimately in charge of the whole of existence and the whole of history is not negotiable, for if he is not, he is not really God at all, and certainly not the God of the Bible.

How can a Good God rule over a Bad World?

However, assertions of that kind can sound not only triumphalist but also rather like whistling in the dark when confronted by our experience of the world we live in. That is why the ideas of the radical theologians have an appeal to thoughtful people. After all, this does not look like a planet ruled (either in broad principle or in minute particulars) by a loving, good and all-powerful God. The great majority of mankind lives in fear, poverty or pain: often, all three. Evil appears to go unchecked, good unrewarded. Natural disasters – earthquakes, floods and tornadoes – bring misery and death. Where is the great and good God? Why – if he is able to do so – does he not intervene? Indeed, further back than that, why did he make it like this in the first place?

It is attractive, in the face of these questions, to abandon the idea of a transcendent, personal God and go either for the interior God (who is part of our inner struggle to make sense of religious and moral values) or for the self-limiting God (who identifies with the human condition but neither causes it nor cures it). It is attractive, but it is not necessary.

After all, these are not new problems for the believer. The world is no worse now than it was in the time of Isaiah, or Jesus, or Augustine, or Aquinas, or Luther. No new discoveries about the universe or human nature have made it more or less difficult to reconcile the idea of a good, infinite and personal God with that of a suffering, flawed humanity. It may be unfashionable to believe in a God set authoritatively over the believer and the creation, but it is not, as we have seen, irrational. Sensitive, thoughtful Christians in the past have reconciled the difficulties, and in so doing have maintained the faith in its full, robust form. There is no good reason why we should not do the same.

The Bible's answer to the dilemma is given in a series of pictures, and it is to these that I now wish to turn. It is important to stress that they are pictures, not propositions: but pictures, I believe, divinely given, part of the self-revelation of God, to enable finite human beings to grasp enough of infinite truth to make sense of the world about us, and our role in it.

The Garden of Eden

The first picture is the Garden of Eden. Here we are confronted by a scenario of innocence and unity. All that God
made is good: the stars and planets, the sky, the good earth
with its seas and lands, the living beings on it in their
profusion of species, the food-bearing plants and trees growing in the rich and co-operative soil. And mankind is also
good, in its two God-given manifestations, man and woman,
enjoying an unspoilt relationship with each other, and with
God himself:

> So God created man in his own image, in the image of God
> he created him; male and female he created them.
>   God blessed them and said to them, 'Be fruitful and
> increase in number; fill the earth and subdue it. Rule over
> the fish of the sea and the birds of the air and over every
> living creature that moves on the ground.'
>   Then God said, 'I give you every seed-bearing plant on
> the face of the whole earth and every tree that has fruit with
> seed in it. They will be yours for food. And to all the beasts
> of the earth and all the birds of the air and all the creatures
> that move on the ground – everything that has the breath
> of life in it – I give every green plant for food.' And it was
> so.
>   God saw all that he had made, and it was very good.[1]

The picture is idyllic, a vision of what we all wish life were
like. But the vision is shattered by the intrusion of evil. God's
adversary, in the guise of a serpent, persuades the woman
and the man to experience evil, as well as good – to 'eat from
the tree of the knowledge of good and evil' (Genesis 2:17). In
that moment, innocence fled. Dire consequences followed:
the end of the idyll. Work – hitherto a joy – became
drudgery. The unspoilt relationship between the man and
the woman, based on their mutual respect and interdepend-
ence, was corrupted into one of dominance and subjugation

('your husband will rule over you'). They were banished from the garden, separated from the 'tree of life', and experienced for the first time the cloud of sin which would obscure their view of God and distort their relationship with him.

To the woman he said,

'I will greatly increase your pains in childbearing, with pain you will give birth to children. Your desire will be for your husband, and he will rule over you.'

To Adam he said, 'Because you listened to your wife and ate from the tree about which I commanded you, "You must not eat of it,"

'Cursed is the ground because of you; through painful toil you will eat of it all the days of your life. It will produce thorns and thistles for you, and you will eat the plants of the field. By the sweat of your brow you will eat your food until you return to the ground, since from it you were taken; for dust you are and to dust you will return.'[2]

And the Lord God said, 'The man has now become like one of us, knowing good and evil. He must not be allowed to reach out his hand and take also from the tree of life and eat, and live for ever.' So the LORD God banished him from the Garden of Eden to work the ground from which he had been taken. After he drove the man out, he placed on the east side of the Garden of Eden cherubim and a flaming sword flashing back and forth to guard the way to the tree of life.[3]

Now this is what Christian theologians call 'the Fall': not the story, but the consequence. God made his world and the people in it good. But he built into it the possibility of moral failure. The human race exploited that possibility, with consequences that are evident in the world around us. We now live as flawed beings in a flawed world.

That rather sweeping summary needs expansion, of course. What does it mean to say that God built into his

creation the possibility of moral failure? Is that to say that
God created, or condones, evil? Is it (as some have suggested)
to imply that God plays immoral tricks on us, teasing us with
a vision of a highway of innocence but preparing moral
obstacles along the way to trip us up? Not at all.

What it means is that human beings are *persons*: not angels,
not automata, but free moral agents. Being made in the
image of God, we have moral autonomy. We are free to
choose: to love and obey God, or to withhold that love and
disobey him. Angels, one assumes, have no choice but to
spend eternity chanting God's praise. We have the choice,
but it is a perilous privilege.

The story of the fruit of the tree of the knowledge of good
and evil explains the problem more tellingly than volumes of
philosophy could do. Right in the middle of human life,
conspicuously and constantly before us, like that splendid
tree, stands moral choice. We are made in the image of God,
but part of that very image is moral freedom: we have to
choose. The initial choice is to experience evil as well as good.
All the rest follows. Being autonomous (not automata), we
wish to assert our independence, but asserting it will eventually, and inevitably, bring us up against the will of God.
The story has a trivial action – eating the fruit – causing
appalling consequences, undreamt of by the hapless offend-
ers. But at the root of that 'trivial' action was a profound act
of defiance: two human beings who wished to assert their
right to make their own choices, including the right to choose
evil. That is, as I am sure it is meant to be, a microcosm of
every act of evil. It is the assertion of *self*.

I think it is important to note at this point that there is a big
difference between saying that God created an environment
in which such a rebellion was possible, and saying that he
planned for it to take place. The difference may seem
academic, especially in the context of a God who is infinite,
and therefore beyond our concept of time. However, God is
not the creator of evil, nor did he plan it for his creatures: that
would be a blasphemous assertion. As St James puts it,

'When tempted, no-one should say, "God is tempting me". For God cannot be tempted by evil, nor does he tempt anyone; but each one is tempted when, by his own evil desire, he is dragged away and enticed' (James 1:13-14). Here the emphasis of sin is placed firmly on self. As self-consciousness and self-awareness are distinctive attributes of humanity, it is not surprising that the human race from the very beginning was in danger of self-indulgence. A person is a being who is self-aware (as God is). It is but a step from that to asserting the absolute autonomy of self: I am master of my fate and captain of my soul. The story of the Garden of Eden and the Fall is a picture of this very process, intrinsically possible from the moment when God created persons: possible, and also, one would have thought, almost inevitable.

The doctrine of the Fall is not a popular one with modern people, but in fact it is consistent with a great deal of what we have come to know about human nature. Of all the great Christian beliefs, it is the most down-to-earth. It meets us where we are and explains why we are there.

In many ways, it is confirmed by our own perception of existence. Doesn't this look like a world created good, but spoiled? Don't human beings look like good people gone wrong? Indeed, don't I find in myself – as St Paul did – this astonishing tension all the while, between something in me that sets high goals and admires what is good, true and holy, and something else that pulls me down, something innately selfish and ugly? The apostle Paul put it starkly: 'When I want to do good, evil is right there with me. For in my inner being I delight in God's law; but I see another law at work in the members of my body, waging war against the law of my mind and making me a prisoner of the law of sin at work within my members. What a wretched man I am! Who will rescue me from this body of death?' (Romans 7:21-24).

The late John A. T. Robinson put this in its historical perspective: 'All men find themselves born into an historical order where sin is there before them, dragging them down.'

We are not the first, in other words, to feel the tension or give way to the temptation. It is – now, at any rate – simply part of being human: made in the image of God, but 'fallen'.

Now the Fall can, and does, go a long way to answering questions about the presence of evil in the world. It says that the possibility of evil was intrinsic in a decision to bring into being autonomous persons – free moral agents – and that its existence is a price God was prepared to pay to achieve that end. The knowledge of good and evil, like the discovery of electricity or nuclear fission, cannot be disinvented. It is now part of the order of things on this planet. Of course, as we shall consider later, God has not simply left mankind to drift on in its moral wilderness. But that tension between good and evil, and especially the insidious downward pull of sin, is a sufficient explanation for the present condition of the human race.

However, it does not, superficially at least, do anything to explain the presence of natural disasters, painful disease or physical deformity in the created order. I realise that some people have tried to argue that sin has led to disease and deformity – not necessarily the sin of the sufferer, but the past sin of the whole human race. There may be something in that, in some cases, but it does not seem either a fair or convincing explanation of most suffering of this kind.

What can be said is that the presence of sin in the human race has introduced a disfunction not just at the individual level, but at the level of whole societies and indeed the planet itself. We are not now what we were meant to be. The planet, too, is not now what it was meant to be. I do not mean that every flood or earthquake is necessarily a consequence of human evil. That would be to misunderstand creation. Many of these 'disasters' are simply natural phenomena, part of the way things are, and of themselves morally neutral. Indeed people suffer through them, as they do through the law of gravity (by falling off a roof) or through the freezing point of water (breaking a leg on an icy patch of road). This is the price of living in an ordered universe – as, indeed, is death itself. Death, in the Christian view, is certainly not of itself evil, but the gateway to life with God. That, at any rate, is St Paul's view. The 'sting of death is sin' (1 Corinthians 15:56) – not death itself, which will bring him to be with Christ. It is the pain and suffering, the bereavement and anger, that strike us as dark clouds across the face of God. It is those reactions themselves, however, that may well be conditioned by sin, perverse consequences of the Fall.

So we have, in the picture of the Garden of Eden, an explanation of the presence of evil in a world created and ruled by a good God. It is not a sign of God's weakness, nor of his indifference either to sin or suffering, but the inevitable consequence of his intention to create self-aware human beings.

The God of the Burning Bush

The second picture I should like to consider is the story of the burning bush, one of the great images of the Old Testament and for many people the classic example of God as 'intervenor'. The Hebrews, the descendants of Abraham, Isaac and Jacob, were captives in Egypt, being pressed into service as slaves in the building of Pharaoh's treasure palaces. The young Jew, Moses, having been rescued from the bulrushes and brought up in Pharaoh's court, found himself in the desert of Midian, at the mountain of Horeb.

There the angel of the LORD appeared to him in flames of fire from within a bush. Moses saw that though the bush was on fire it did not burn up. So Moses thought, 'I will go over and see this strange sight – why the bush does not burn up.'

When the LORD saw that he had gone over to look, God called to him from within the bush, 'Moses, Moses!'

And Moses said, 'Here I am.'

'Do not come any closer,' God said. 'Take off your

sandals, for the place where you are standing is holy ground.' Then he said, 'I am the God of your fathers, the God of Abraham, the God of Isaac and the God of Jacob.' At this, Moses hid his face, because he was afraid to look at God.

The LORD said, 'I have indeed seen the misery of my people in Egypt. I have heard them crying out because of their slave drivers, and I am concerned about their suffering. So I have come down to rescue them from the hand of the Egyptians and to bring them up out of that land into a good and spacious land, a land flowing with milk and honey – the home of the Canaanites, Hittites, Amorites, Perizzites, Hivites and Jebusites. And now the cry of the Israelites has reached me and I have seen the way the Egyptians are oppressing them. So now, go. I am sending you to Pharaoh to bring my people the Israelites out of Egypt.'

But Moses said to God, 'Who am I, that I should go to Pharaoh and bring the Israelites out of Egypt?'

And God said, 'I will be with you. And this will be the sign to you that it is I who have sent you: When you have brought the people out of Egypt, you will worship God on this mountain.'

Moses said to God, 'Suppose I go to the Israelites and say to them. "The God of your fathers has sent me to you," and they ask me, "What is his name?" Then what shall I tell them?'

God said to Moses, 'I am who I am. This is what you are to say to the Israelites. "I AM has sent me to you."'[4]

This story is unique on a number of levels. In the first place, it marks a great leap forward in God's revelation of himself, because here he reveals for the first time the divine name, 'I AM' – 'Jehovah', as the title has been wrongly known to Christians, or more correctly 'YAHWEH', though no one can be sure how the consonants by which the name was rendered in Hebrew are to be pronounced. The point is that the God who had been content to be known as the 'God of Abraham, Isaac and Jacob' – in other words, the 'tribal God' of Israel – was in fact an infinite personal being, without beginning or ending, a kind of permanent present tense. 'I AM' simply speaks of a being who exists in his own right, independent of his creatures or his creation, the God of Abraham only in the sense that Abraham acknowledged him, and emphatically not in the sense that Abraham authenticated him. This God does not need human beings to prove or justify his existence. He *exists*. He *is*. That is as clear a picture of the transcendence of God as we are given in the Bible. Indeed, so awe-inspiring was this revelation that it transformed the religion of Israel for the rest of its history.

On the other hand, the God so transcendently revealed in the burning bush was not a distant or remote being. He was, indeed, infinite – 'I AM' – but he was personal – 'The God of your fathers'. And he was also involved in our human condition:

> The LORD said, 'I have indeed seen the misery of my people in Egypt. I have heard them crying out because of their slave drivers, and I am concerned about their suffering. So I have come down to rescue them from the hand of the Egyptians . . . And now the cry of the Israelites has reached me, and I have seen the way the Egyptians are oppressing them. So now, go. I am sending you to Pharaoh to bring my people the Israelites out of Egypt.'[5]

These are the words of an immanent God: 'I have *seen* the misery of my people . . . I have *heard* them crying . . . I am *concerned* about their suffering . . . I have *come down* to rescue them.' So even in a picture of glory and holiness ('Do not come any closer . . . Take off your sandals') we are shown God as identifying with his suffering creatures. The two pictures are not mutually exclusive. Moses was in awe of this amazing sight: the bush was on fire but it was not consumed. And yet out of the flames the voice that spoke was the voice of mercy and compassion. There is no clearer picture in the Old Testament of the nature of God, who is infinite and holy, and yet personal and accessible. This one incident, in a way, is the most eloquent rebuttal of the idea that there is some inherent incompatibility between the God above us and the God within us.

There is a further point. The notion of an 'internalised' God – 'the religious requirement personified', in Cupitt's words – may solve the occasional intellectual problem, but it solves nothing else. Especially, it leaves human beings without any source of help outside themselves. If all we can call upon, in our time of desperate need, is a personified religious requirement, then we really are on our own in the universe. The God within, in other words, is meaningless unless he is able to *do* something.

The story of the burning bush – however we interpret it – speaks of a moment in the history of Israel, and in the life of Moses, when God intervened. His intervention – literally, his coming into things from outside – arose out of his involvement with his covenant people, but it was effective because he had the power to alter events and people. The events, like the Passover and the crossing of the Red Sea, were altered by his authority and power as Creator. The people, like Moses, were altered by his interior authority and power as Redeemer.

There seems no reasonable doubt that something very remarkable happened to bring the Hebrews out of Egypt. However much some may argue that the narrative was subsequently embellished, the liberation of an enslaved people and their eventual resettlement in a hostile neighbouring territory sounds like a remarkable achievement. Throughout their long history the Jews have ascribed it to the intervention of Yahweh. The 'event' is now, of course, thoroughly 'internalised' in the religious experience of Judaism, but that does not mean that it was not rooted in an actual, historical event, a moment in history when God demonstrated the inherent authority of a Creator over his creation.

The prophet Jeremiah expressed this authority in the picture of the potter, shaping and reshaping the clay to his own design:

> This is the word that came to Jeremiah from the LORD: 'Go down to the potter's house, and there I will give you my message.' So I went down to the potter's house, and I saw him working at the wheel. But the pot he was shaping from the clay was marred in his hands; so the potter formed it into another pot, shaping it as seemed best to him.
>
> Then the word of the LORD came to me: 'O house of Israel, can I not do with you as this potter does?' declares the LORD. 'Like clay in the hand of the potter, so are you in my hand, O house of Israel.'[6]

St Paul developed the same metaphor:

> Shall what is formed say to him who formed it, 'Why did you make me like this?' Does not the potter have the right to make out of the same lump of clay some pottery for noble purposes and some for common use?[7]

Again, however much modern people may dislike the idea, if we are created beings, rather than cosmic accidents, our Creator has rights as well as we do, and one of those rights, according to the biblical picture of God, is the right to intervene, like the potter reshaping the clay. An internalised and powerless God may suit the modern intellectual scenario (though I doubt very much whether it does), but such a 'God' is of little use in the real world of pain, conflict, temptation and fear. We may by all means believe that God stands with us, and within us, in our deepest human needs. But we may also believe that, because he is infinitely above us, he can actually do something about them. The message from the burning bush was not, 'I have heard your cry. I share your pain. I suffer with you. But you must go on suffering, because there is nothing I can do to alter it.' The message was altogether different. 'I have heard your cry. I share your pain. I suffer with you. *So I have come down to rescue you from the land of the Egyptians*' (Exodus 3:8).

It is true that that rescue was to be achieved through a human agent, Moses. It was the power of God 'internalised' in him that would prove the decisive factor in bringing the Hebrews out. The two things – the power and presence of God – were, as ever, inextricably linked. 'What God has joined together let no one put asunder' (Mark 10:9).

The Baby of Bethlehem

The third 'picture' I should like to offer to illustrate the biblical balance between the concept of a God 'over' us and a God 'within' us is the most familiar of all to most people: the birth of Jesus. Here, for many Christians, is the supreme picture of God 'intervening' in human affairs. Indeed, the coming of Jesus has often been portrayed in books and sermons as the invasion of an alien, rebel planet by the Prince of the Universe. Medieval carols and modern Gospel choruses have perpetuated the idea of a kind of divine D-Day, when God 'sent' his Son to take on Satan, defeat him, and release his people of the new covenant just as Moses released his people of the old one.

Many modern theologians have reacted to this view of the incarnation, rejecting the whole idea of a divine 'invasion' of planet Earth. They prefer to stress the undoubted truth that God did not 'come to us' in Jesus because he had never been away; that he did not 'invade' a 'rebel' planet because he was already the King over the Kings of the earth; and that the important thing about Jesus is that he was 'one of us' rather than a Superman from another world.

But the picture the New Testament gives, in the stories in

Matthew and Luke about the birth of Jesus, avoids both of these extreme views. On the one hand, it does not see the coming of Jesus as an 'invasion' of earth from outside. But at the same time it is quite clear that Jesus – although undoubtedly 'one of us' – is uniquely different from us.

At the heart of the biblical story of the coming of Jesus is, of course, the virgin birth – or, more correctly, the virginal conception. Again, it is not a very popular doctrine today. Many Christians and many theologians have written it off as a retrospective bit of image-boosting for Jesus, developed in the third and fourth centuries, to assure him a status at least equal to a number of rival pagan divinities, masculine and feminine. This writing-off is convenient, because of all the New Testament miracles this one most disturbs the presuppositions of modern people, by appearing to suggest that coitus may not be the most significant thing in the universe and because it makes it impossible to regard Jesus as no more than a very good, inspired and prophetic man, whom we can cope with, rather than the divine Son of God, carrying an unacceptable degree of authority.

The insight this narrative affords does not depend on whether the virginal conception is something that actually happened, as a matter of biological fact, or whether it is a picture given by divine inspiration to light up for us the true identity of Jesus. To argue – as I shall later – that the Bible is inspired by God is not to deny any possibility that it conveys truth through symbol and allegory as well as through factual history.

However – and in passing – I do think that much of the debunking of the virginal conception stems from philosophical presuppositions rather than from the evidence. It is certainly *not* true that it was a third or fourth century invention. It is there in the Gospels, after all – certainly written by AD 80 – and presented (at any rate in Luke's Gospel) not as parable but as reportage. Clearly the apostolic Church believed it, and it is worth remembering that among their number was a certain Mary of Nazareth, the only person who has ever lived who knows the truth of the matter. She had no reason to invent the story so long after the event, and in any case all we know of her suggests she would not be the sort of person to promote a deliberate deception. Yet it is most likely that Luke met her, at Ephesus, and it is certain that the Jerusalem Church – generally thought to be a major source for the First Gospel – knew her well: she was a founding member. How could the belief in the virginal conception of Jesus have established itself in Jerusalem and Ephesus, in 'Matthew' and 'Luke', if she had denied it?

Faced with these considerations, it is not so easy to argue that the whole idea was a later embellishment. Within the lifetime of the people principally involved the virginal conception was believed by Christians. Add to that certain obscure but interesting references elsewhere in the New Testament[8], and you will see why it is not so readily dismissed as unhistorical.

Be that as it may – and, as I said, it does not greatly affect my argument – the account of the 'Annunciation' in Luke's Gospel is a picture of God's relationship to the world parallel to the story of the burning bush:

In the sixth month, God sent the angel Gabriel to Nazareth, a town in Galilee, to a virgin pledged to be married to a man named Joseph, a descendant of David. The virgin's name was Mary. The angel went to her and said, 'Greetings, you who are highly favoured! The Lord is with you.'

Mary was greatly troubled at his words and wondered what kind of greeting this might be. But the angel said to her, 'Do not be afraid, Mary, you have found favour with God. You will be with child and give birth to a son, and you are to give him the name Jesus. He will be great and will be called the Son of the Most High. The Lord God will give him the throne of his father David, and he will reign over the house of Jacob for ever; his kingdom will never end.'

'How will this be,' Mary asked the angel, 'since I am a virgin?'

The angel answered, 'The Holy Spirit will come upon you, and the power of the Most High will overshadow you. So the holy one to be born will be called the Son of God.'[9]

Once again, as in Exodus, we have God's people in distress. The Jews had been under foreign domination, Greek and Roman, for three hundred years. Once again, God moves to help them – to 'restore the throne of David'. But this time, he goes further. He used Moses as a means to bring about his purpose, by speaking and acting through him. Mary, however, is to be used as the means of bringing his Son into the world: 'the Holy Spirit will come upon you, and the power of the most High will overshadow you. So the holy one to be born will be called the Son of God.' Mary was not herself to be the deliverer, as Moses was, but she was to be the human means by which the deliverer would come.

In Luke's story, the Holy Spirit 'came upon' Mary. The resulting conception was both human and divine; and the baby who resulted from it was human and divine: not, as is sometimes suggested, half human and half divine, but fully both, a perfect fusion – as every baby is – of the characteristics of both parents. So Jesus becomes the perfect Saviour for the human race. He is divine (on his Father's side, as we might say) and so can perfectly represent God to the human race. He is human (on his mother's side) and so can perfectly represent us to God. He 'understands' God and he 'understands' us. Through him, true communication can take place.

The value of the virginal conception for us is that it illuminates the whole idea of incarnation. It preserves the special identity of Jesus, while emphasising his unity with the human race. It expresses clearly that God acted, at a point in history, to liberate the whole of mankind, but puts that action firmly into the heart of human existence and experience. It was not an invasion so much as an infiltration. God, in Jesus, entered human nature: 'the Word was made flesh.' But he did not come as an alien: 'that was the true light that gives light to every man'. God was always near us, but in the incarnation that truth took a visible expression. He 'became like us'. No, more than that, he *became* us. He 'took our very nature' (Philippians 2:7), not as an outsider, like a space visitor in a science fiction story, but as one who was and had always been a person and expressed perfectly what human nature imperfectly mirrors. In other words, we mistake the incarnation if we view it solely from a human perspective: God became man. In fact, the creation story tells us that mankind is made in the image of God, and what the birth of Jesus achieved was to restore, in one person, what God had originally intended, that his 'image' should be visible in his creation. And what he achieved in Jesus as a prototype he intends also to achieve in all those who through Jesus are reborn in his likeness. St Paul expresses it like this:

> For since death came through a man, the resurrection of the dead comes also through a man. For as in Adam all die, so in Christ all will be made alive.[10]

Now all of this may sound obscure and even academic. But the story of the birth at Bethlehem earths it. This is no obscure doctrine, but a narrative as human and compelling as any ever told. An ordinary couple make their way to a far-off town where in the simplest and plainest of settings a baby is born. But that birth has two unique elements. The first is the mother's claim that the child was conceived not through normal intercourse with a man, but by the direct operation of the Holy Spirit. The second is that the actual birth was announced by angels: not in a palace, but on the hillsides where shepherds – social outcasts, as they were seen at the time – were looking after their flocks. This birth, then, was for all the people, not just a chosen and pious few.

The 'meaning' of that first unique element we have already touched upon. It marked out the child as both human and divine. Jesus not only bore the image of God as all human beings do, but he bore it untainted by the evil that has distorted human nature since the Fall. He was human, and his birth was, so far as we know, completely normal. But he was also divine, showing us in one person what God is like and what human beings were meant to be. That is, of course, a staggering claim, and it is not really surprising that many people baulk at it. However, the more one studies and absorbs the life and teaching of Jesus the less incredible it becomes.

Similarly the incarnation – the coming into history of Jesus – makes sense in terms of the understanding of God presented by the Bible as a whole. What I mean is that this is exactly how one would have expected God to act – not in an 'invasion', not by manipulating events, not by overturning human freedom or moral autonomy, but by involving himself totally in our condition. In a way, it takes the picture of the burning bush one stage further. Then, God identified with his people by 'ordaining' a human agent, Moses, to act in his name. Now, at Bethlehem, God identified with his people by entering into the human predicament himself, through his Son, Jesus.

I realise that that statement itself raises all kinds of problems, some of which we shall be looking at. Certainly it is a huge jump from the idea of an objectively real, personal but infinite God, who is not only the intelligence behind existence itself but the creative power of the universe, to a belief that God 'took human form', which is how the incarnation is usually expressed. But at least the Old Testament model of the Exodus establishes a precedent of a less mind-blowing kind. It shows God – infinite and personal, the 'God of Abraham, Isaac and Jacob' but also the great 'I AM' – involving himself intimately in the condition of his human creatures. It is not *such* a vast step from Mount Horeb to Bethlehem.

4   HAS GOD 'SPOKEN'?

One of the really fascinating things about working in religious broadcasting in a multi-cultural society is the way it sharpens the distinction between fundamental and peripheral questions. More and more people are realising that the most important religious question after 'Is there a God?' is 'Has he spoken?' It is closely followed by two more: 'If he has, how or where has he spoken?' and 'What has he said?'

Christianity itself is divided by these questions. Conservative Protestants and traditional Catholics answer 'yes' to the first question, but divide over the second and third. Liberal Protestants answer 'no' (though undoubtedly qualified in many ways) to the first, and therefore do not regard the second and third as very interesting. For them, it is man's search for God, truth, understanding or reality, that matters. The notion of some revealed deposit of truth capable of fulfilling that search seems to them an illusion, a dangerous chimera.

The same divisions occur in other religions. Jews and Muslims answer 'yes' to the first question but begin to divide over the second and third. For Buddhists and Hindus the answer to the first is very similar to that of liberal Protestants, and so is their attitude to the third and fourth.

There is little doubt that, so far as Christendom is concerned, the overwhelming answer of the Church has always been 'yes' to the first question. The writer to the Hebrews, in the first century, put it like this:

In the past God spoke to our forefathers through the prophets at many times and in various ways, but in these last days he has spoken to us by his Son.[1]

There is a reassuring rationality in the idea of a God who 'speaks'. If, as we have been thinking, there is an objectively real, personal, infinite God, who is good, then it seems to me absolutely essential that he should in some way explain himself to the personal but finite creatures he has made. Not to do so would be evil, a malign and terrifying act of deception.

Human beings are aware not only of their environment but of their own existence. We come to self-consciousness slowly, but really. Even as children we know our identity, and begin to ask questions. 'Who am I?' 'Where do I come from?' 'What is the purpose of my being here?'

We also quickly realise that we are finite, mortal. All around us people die, the precious gift which seems to mean so much taken away like the shallow gasp of air that marks its passing. Night falls, the darkness closes in. There are dreams and imaginings, fears we cannot pin down to words, hopes and joys we cannot explain but are terrified of losing – most of all, the precious but devastating experience of love, in which we put our happiness in the hands of someone else.

There is so much we can never discover for ourselves, however efficiently we analyse our environment and master its laws. But most of all, there is the only question that really matters in the end: Is there any purpose in our existence? If we are merely chemical accidents, caught on some temporary beach-head in a silent, dead and purposeless universe, then there is nothing to do but make the best of it, and stave off oblivion for as long as we can.

But if, as most people have always believed, that is an incredible and untenable view of our position – if life as we see it and experience it simply does not *feel* like a purposeless accident – then that most fundamental question of all returns with irresistible insistence. If there is a purpose in life, who can tell us what it is except the intelligence that planned it? If we cannot find it out, because it is literally beyond us, then we are thrown back on the only other reasonable proposition: it must be revealed to us.

That word 'must' deserves further consideration. It is hard to say of a being of infinite power and intelligence that it 'must' do anything. Yet there are some moral 'musts' that seem to follow inevitably from the concept of a *good* God. He *must* oppose evil. He *must* will the ultimate good of his creatures. And he *must* tell the truth. If he does not oppose evil, does not will our ultimate good, and either distorts or conceals the truth, then he is not good.

The important word there, in this argument, is 'conceals'. It might be argued that God is under no obligation to tell us anything, that he has a right to keep us 'in the dark', so to speak. But for me that is a denial of his goodness. To leave us floundering and frightened in an unexplained and inexplicable existence is a kind of refined mental torture wholly inconsistent with the notion of a good and loving God. If he knows the truth (and he must), and if he can reveal it (and he can), then not to do so is, quite simply, cruel.

So we arrive at the notion of God as communicator: the idea that if there is a good God then he must reveal to his personal creatures enough truth to enable them to make sense of their own existence, of their own environment, and of the God who made them. In other words, the infinite-personal God is a God who 'speaks'.

That leads us to the second question. If God 'speaks', how and where has he spoken? The writer of the letter to the Hebrews, already quoted, said that he spoke 'to our forefathers through the prophets . . . in various ways', but 'in these last days he has spoken to us by his Son.' St Paul, writing to the church at Rome, says that God has also spoken through our consciences, which 'bear witness' to his moral standards, and through what he has created: 'What may be known about God is plain to them (that is, to godless and wicked men), because God has made it plain. For since the creation of the world God's invisible qualities – his eternal power and divine nature – have been clearly seen, being understood from what he has made.'[2]

Now clearly there are two different kinds of revelation here. To say that God has 'spoken' through creation is not the same thing as to say that he has 'spoken' through people, whether prophets or a Son. According to Paul, what God has 'made plain' through the created world is 'his eternal power and divine nature'. That is to say, anyone looking at the world around them – a world of order, of awesome immensity – would be compelled to admit that it was the work of a divine being of infinite power. But that conclusion has to be drawn from the evidence. It has to be 'understood', in Paul's words. And while it may indeed have been self-evident in the ancient world, where no other explanation of the physical universe was on offer, it would be hard to say in the modern world that people are 'compelled' to understand or interpret the evidence in that way. The argument from creation is strong: stronger, perhaps, than most of us have thought in modern times. But it is not irresistible or irrefutable. For us today, at least, it needs the interpretation and reinforcement of a further revelation. We want – perhaps, need – God to *explain* it to us.

It seems to me that the second form of revelation – God speaking to us through people – is therefore the more important one. Left to our own devices, the ingenuity of the human brain will find all kinds of explanations for the physical universe other than that it was created by a divine being of eternal power. They do not need to be especially convincing to achieve their objective, which is to provide alternatives to the previously universal belief that 'in the beginning God created the heavens and the earth'.

So, 'at many times and in various ways', as Hebrews puts it, 'God spoke to our forefathers through the prophets'. God himself, it is claimed, reinforced the evidence of the visible, physical world with a verbal revelation. He 'explained himself'.

Who were these 'prophets' and how were they recognised? At least as far back as Abraham, who is described as a 'prophet', the Bible records the words and actions of these people. The Old Testament uses three different titles for them. Sometimes a Hebrew word is used which implies that God's words boiled or bubbled up inside them – the prophet is a speaker of divine oracles, almost without knowing it. Another Hebrew word, usually translated 'seer', is the earlier name for a prophet, and this seems to emphasise a gift for seeing and, perhaps, interpreting visions and dreams. The third title given to the prophet is 'Man of God', which concerns his relationship with God – the words which 'bubbled up' or the visions which he saw were not self-induced, but came out of a specially close relationship between Yahweh and himself.

It is this relationship which distinguishes the true prophets, the 'Men of God', from the false prophets, who were legion in the history of Israel. They might all begin their oracles with the phrase, 'Thus says the Lord', but those who were not 'Men of God' were disqualified from speaking his word. Of course, the only objective test of this was in the results. False prophecies are, by their very nature, eventually proved to be just that, and not only in the strictly predictive aspect of prophecy. Time and again, as in the case of Jeremiah, the true prophet spoke a very unpopular 'word of the Lord', but it was eventually demonstrated to be both a true analysis of a present plight and a true prediction of its eventual outcome. Jeremiah is vindicated as a man who spoke the truth about his own time, and hence – and this is important – we take seriously the things he spoke about the wider matters of the nature and purposes of God. The false prophets, so numerous and influential in their day, are forgotten. They were proved to be wrong, and that is one thing a prophet cannot afford to be.

The great prophets of Israel stand as a line, stretching back at least to Abraham, of divine revelation through human instruments. They were human, not infallible. Sometimes the vision is confused and confusing. Sometimes it is so 'internal' to the prophet that the reader can only guess at its meaning. Sometimes it is a statement of utterly compelling majesty, a vision of the good which is totally universal:

> They will beat their swords into ploughshares
> And their spears into pruning hooks.
> Nation will not take up sword against nation,
> Nor will they train for war any more . . .[3]

But, just as the 'revelation' through creation is limited by our ability or willingness to see it, so the revelation through human prophets is limited by their human limitations and by our ability to understand and interpret what they were saying. The apostle Peter captures something of this sense of clouded mystery as he looks back at the prophets of Israel from the perspective of the New Testament:

> Concerning this salvation, the prophets, who spoke of the grace that was to come to you, searched intently and with the greatest care, trying to find out the time and circumstances to which the Spirit of Christ in them was pointing when he predicted the sufferings of Christ and the glories that would follow. It was revealed to them that they were not serving themselves but you, when they spoke of the things that have now been told you by those who have preached the gospel to you by the Holy Spirit sent from heaven. Even angels long to look into these things.[4]

The prophets in the Bible were not only 'Men of God' but also men of their time. The revelation of God through them was fragmentary – the New English Bible translation of 'at many times' in the opening sentence of Hebrews. The pieces have to be gathered up, sorted, assembled and analysed. The prophets of Israel give a picture of God which is impressive and convincing, but it is not the whole picture, and it is not easily accessible to their readers. They are recounting for us, in pictures, stories and poetry, an inner vision, an internal revelation given to them at a certain time in history and place in geography. But it is their vision, not ours, and it is rooted in a point of time – *their* time.

The eternal dimension is also there, of course. The prophets were not simply isolated individuals, but part of a prophetic stream that has flowed through human experience, even before biblical times, and far beyond the boundaries of the Jewish religion. Of this broader prophetic stream the mysterious Balaam, whose story is told in the book of Numbers, may stand as a representative. In ordinary language he was a soothsayer, yet Yahweh revealed something of himself to this pagan 'seer'. His experience thus becomes part of this long, if fragmented, process of God's revelation of himself to mankind through mankind. It is as though the truth of God is constantly flowing through human experience like an underground stream, searching for places and people where, like a spring, it can burst out into the open. The prophets – all of those people who have been close to God and seen visions or heard words of truth – are like spiritual oases in the desert of history.

But the writer of the letter to the Hebrews does not stop with the prophets. They spoke 'at many times and in various ways', but 'in these last days' – that is, in what we now call the first century AD – 'he has spoken to us by his Son'. The underground stream, to pursue the analogy, has finally surfaced. In the words of Jesus himself, he is the 'fountain of living water'. No longer is God speaking in a fragmentary way through intermediaries. God has now spoken through his Son, a personal ambassador able to declare the full truth about him, to show us his very nature and explain to us his very purposes. That, at any rate, was how the apostolic Church saw it.

But was it also how Jesus saw it? Certainly he saw himself, as his contemporaries saw him, as a prophet:

'Only in his home town and in his own house is a prophet without honour.'[5]

'Surely no prophet can die outside Jerusalem.'[6]

To the people and to the disciples Jesus was a 'prophet powerful in word and deed' (Luke 24:19).

In fact, some – again, including the disciples – were for a time inclined to believe he was a 'reincarnation' of Elijah or John the Baptist, great prophets of the distant or recent past. But later they came to believe that Jesus was 'more than a prophet'.

In his parable of the vineyard, Jesus depicted the people of Israel – or at any rate their religious leaders – as being like dishonest tenants who killed or humiliated all the landlord's messengers (the prophets) until finally they even killed the last emissary, his Son.

For Jesus, the coming of himself as the Son was the end of that long prophetic line. I think the case is irresistible that he saw himself as more than a prophet, 'one greater than Jonah' (Luke 11:32), in his own words.

We shall be looking at the arguments about the nature of Jesus in a later chapter. Certainly we need to be aware that there is more than one way of understanding the title 'Son of God'. But the unanimous testimony of all the New Testament witnesses is that Jesus was seen by his followers – and, more importantly, saw himself – as a divine ambassador, speaking in the name of God in a way that even the prophets of Israel had not claimed to do.

So God speaks. He communicates with us. The Christian God is not a secret deity, veiling his identity or his purposes, but a God of disclosure, who actually wants his creatures to know their Creator. This is a fundamental truth about him, and it seems to me entirely in keeping with the concept of an infinite, personal God. It is not strange that God has spoken to the human race. In fact, it would have been stranger if he had not.

5 GOD AS COMMUNICATOR

It is one thing to claim that God has spoken through the prophets and, finally, through his Son. It is another, and rather more practical, question to ask how people living today can have reliable access to whatever it was he said.

I began the last chapter with three questions. 'Has God spoken?' – to which I should unambiguously answer 'yes'. 'If so, how or where has he spoken?' – to which I have answered, 'Through creation, through conscience, through the prophets and through his Son.' The third question was, 'What has he said?' – to which I reserve my answer for a later chapter. For the present it is that second question ('How or where has he spoken?') and its answer which I wish to examine more closely. For as I have just suggested, it is not much use knowing how and where God has spoken if we do not have access to what he has said here and now. The prophets are dead. Jesus lived and taught nearly two thousand years ago. How can what God said through them reach me today? In what way does God 'speak' to us?

The most obvious answer, though not the only one, is 'Through the Bible'. There, Christians claim, is the record of God's dealings with his people over the ages. There are the words of the prophets, and the words and actions of Jesus. Turn to the pages of the Bible, many people will say, and God speaks *now* through what he has said in the past. The word spoken in creation, spoken through prophets and spoken through his 'living Word', Jesus, becomes a written

Word, available to all people at all times, uncorrupted and incorruptible.

That, at any rate, is the theory. The problem – and it is a serious one – lies in the very nature of communication. It is a subject that has fascinated me all through my own working life. I began as a school-teacher, trying to 'communicate' ideas about the right and effective use of English, the appreciation of English literature, and what was laughingly called 'religious knowledge'. Then I became a magazine journalist, trying to 'communicate' information, ideas and arguments through the medium of print. And then – in roughly the last third of my working life – I moved into the electronic media, and spent my time trying to 'communicate' the same sort of things through radio and television.

In my first career I was engaging in what is called 'interpersonal' communication. I knew my pupils, they knew me, and all the subtleties of human relationships could be employed to ensure that what they were receiving was as nearly as possible what I was 'transmitting'. A lifted eyebrow, a pause, a grin, a good laugh together – all of these were part of the communication process. I could only communicate with a very few people – thirty or so at a time, perhaps two hundred in all in the course of a week – but the communication was relatively efficient and the influence I had on them quite profound. That is not boasting, incidentally. For good or ill, we have all been profoundly influenced by those who taught us when we were young: sometimes unconsciously, sometimes unwillingly. Occasionally I meet or hear from old pupils of mine, and I am surprised and sometimes quite worried by the degree of influence I had on them. Interpersonal communication, for all its imperfections, remains by far the best human beings can manage. We still misunderstand and misinterpret each other, but there is the *possibility* of very good communication. What we are trying to convey and what they are managing to receive are often pretty close or even almost identical.

Radio, and especially television, are extensions of inter-

personal communication. Through technology we have
made it possible to create a one-way relationship that has
many similarities to normal human social intercourse.
Through the voice (alone, in radio) and the image of a face
(on television) one person or a group of people can communicate to individuals or groups far away. It is 'mass' communication in so far as millions can hear or see it, but it is
individual and personal in the sense that each person hears or
sees it for themselves, often alone in a room or a car.

As a means of communication it shares many of the
features of interpersonal communication. Words, inflec-
tions, pauses, tone of voice (on radio), and expressions,
grimaces and gestures (on television) are similar. The viewer
at home may well *feel* that almost perfect communication is
taking place, but in fact it is always flawed by the fact that it is
one-way. *We* see or hear the broadcaster; the broadcaster
cannot see or hear us. He or she has to imagine an audience,
but that audience is invisible and untouchable. The speaker
is not, however hard he tries, speaking to me, but to an
anonymous crowd. I cannot influence him, or indicate by
expression, gesture or word that I have not understood, or
that I share his enthusiasm, or that at this or that point he has
failed to carry me with him. As a method of mass communication it is highly efficient, but as a medium it is not as
effective as interpersonal communication, and can never
be.

Print moves the process further away from the personal.
Now there is not even the human voice, let alone the image of
a human face. All that is left to communicate our ideas are the
words – written symbols representing on paper the sounds
we make when human beings communicate with each other.
Words are marvellous things, of course, but in normal
speech they are only part of the process of communication.
The single word 'well' in English, which is often no more
than a signal that we are about to start the transmission of
ideas, can convey half a dozen different meanings according
to its context, the inflection of the voice or even the facial

expression that accompanies it. It can be an ejaculation of surprise, disapproval or satisfaction. It can be a precise description of degree of achievement ('How did she do in her German test?'). It can inject doubt into an otherwise apparently unambiguous sentence ('Well, I would have thought he was an honest man'). And it can also, of course, be a noun denoting a water-hole bored in the ground.

By now you may be wondering what all of this has to do with the process of divine communication through creation, the prophets, Jesus, and the Bible. The answer is, a great deal. If a personal God wished to communicate with his personal creatures, he would presumably use every available medium to do so, and thus ensure the most accurate and effective transmission of the truth he wished to convey.

Human beings receive information in various ways. Most effectively, as we have seen, we learn through interpersonal contact – not simply speech, but all the other nuances of non-verbal communication. We learn through experience: the things we see, hear and feel, the events of our lives, the difficulties we encounter and overcome. Since the advent of writing, we also learn through the written word, which can communicate across history, passing on the exact words (if not always the exact *ideas*) of previous generations, across boundaries of language, culture and time.

God communicates in each of these ways, as we should expect. He speaks to us through our experience of life and our environment: 'God's invisible qualities have been clearly seen, being understood from what has been made' (Romans 1:20). He speaks to us through our moral feelings and sensibilities – what we call 'conscience': 'The requirements of the law are written on their hearts, their consciences also bearing witness' (Romans 2:15). He has spoken to us through the prophets, whose words and actions have become part of the experience of the human race. He spoke to us, best of all, in an interpersonal way, through his Son Jesus – not simply in the words he used but also in that intensely human form of communication made up of every aspect of person-to-person relationship: facial expressions, tone of voice, laughter, gesture, touch, embrace, eye-contact and so on. The sheer intensity of the communication Jesus achieved during his brief three-year ministry can still be felt, albeit at second-hand, through the Gospels, and it probably accounts for the enormous impact they have made on succeeding generations, even though separated from the actual event by centuries of history, thousands of miles and a yawning culture-gap.

There is the crux of the matter; it looks as though all of this 'communication' happened in the past, *except* the written record of it. An interested unbeliever might feel a sense of deprivation. God spoke through the prophets. God even established interpersonal communication with us through Jesus. And all we have today is the written record of it.

But that would be seriously to distort the picture. Let us take that last sentence and instead of using it as a negative statement ('all we have') use it as the base of a communication pyramid. *We have today a reliable written record of the life, words and actions of Jesus.* That is a very good base for the pyramid. Even allowing for the problems of translation – the Gospels, for instance, almost certainly give us a Greek translation of the original Aramaic words Jesus spoke – and of cultural conditioning, we have in our hands, as we have seen, a powerful and moving picture of the Son of God on earth. We shall come back to this later, and I have dealt with it more fully in another book[1], but I think we may assume that the impact the written record has on the modern reader is of the same kind as the historical Jesus had on the contemporary people who actually met him. That, in itself, is a sort of miracle.

We also have the words of the prophets of Israel, which provide an historical background and context to the life of Jesus and have great value in themselves as vehicles of truth about God. And we have the writings of the early Church, recording the impact the 'Jesus event' had on the first and second generation of his followers, both those who actually met him 'in the flesh' and those who believed because of their testimony.

So much for the written record, which I see as the broad bottom section of the pyramid of God's communication to the human race.

Above it stretches all that human experience which I mentioned earlier: our perception and interpretation of the world around us, our moral feelings through conscience, our sharing in the spiritual dimension of life. This part of the pyramid is less precise than that which is written, but the important thing is that it is based on it, not independent of it. Everything human beings have thought about creation has not been correct, of course. We do not worship the local mountain, or the moon, or a wooded grove. All spiritual experiences are not equally valid. We do not endorse the occult, or spirit-worship. Even conscience can be unreliable, because cultural conditioning can blunt our sensitivity. We do not offer human sacrifices, or believe that God endorses slavery.

Our test is the written record. We interpret all of these means of communication by the only record we have of God's ultimate communication in Jesus – the account we have of him in the Bible. That is confirmed and endorsed by the experience of the Christian community, the Church, but even that community cannot rewrite the record.

But there is one further factor in this whole matter of how and where God communicates with us today. The Nicene Creed puts it like this:

> I believe in the Holy Spirit,
> The Lord, the giver of life,
> Who spoke through the prophets . . .

I realise it may seem to the sceptic that I have suddenly introduced a new and irrational element into the argument, like an old-time conjurer producing a rabbit from his top-hat to crown an indifferent performance. The Holy Spirit does tend to have that effect on any debate about theology. When finally cornered, Christians tend to produce him with a flourish and 'with one mighty leap our hero escapes'. 'Ah,' we say, 'but that's where the Holy Spirit comes into it.' It is a statement that brooks no contradiction.

However, and having said all that, it simply will not do to leave the Holy Spirit out of the argument for fear of appearing to introduce an irrational or mystical element into it. The 'Spirit of God' is an essential element in the religious history of the Bible from the second sentence of Genesis ('And the Spirit of God was hovering over the waters') to the penultimate paragraph of Revelation ('And the Spirit and the bride say "Come!"'). He is seen as the evidence of God at work in human experience, as the executive agent of Yahweh, as the insistent moving force – his name both in Hebrew and Greek means 'wind' or 'breath' – of God's purposes in the world. He is seen all through the Bible as the divine interpreter of God's will.

That role has two sides, as it does for any interpreter. The first is to understand as completely as possible what the originator wishes to convey. The second is to interpret or translate it in such a way that the recipient understands as completely as possible what the originator intended. It is always a difficult process, fraught with pitfalls. But the divine interpreter has worked away at it over the centuries, ceaselessly refining the interpretation, guarding it from corruption or distortion, and operating (if I may put it this way) both within the mind of God, to understand his purpose, and within the mind of human beings to make it as clear as possible to them.

That is why the Holy Spirit is seen as the ultimate author of the Scriptures, working through their various human authors to ensure that the total picture they give is a true one. But he is also seen as at work in the Church, interpreting those same Scriptures within the community of faith, and within the individual Christian, too, to make the communication true and effective. The whole pyramid of God's communication with us, in other words, is impregnated with the activity of the Holy Spirit. He is the guarantor of its authenticity and trustworthiness.

In practice, it is this operation of the Holy Spirit that distinguishes the Christian Scriptures from other sacred writings, and the Christian revelation as a whole from other credal systems. The God of the Bible is, as we have seen, a God who wishes to reveal himself to his creatures; he is a God who speaks. But this revelation – whether through creation, the prophets, his Son Jesus, or the record of these experiences, words and actions in the Bible – has its unity in the all-pervasive Holy Spirit who is at work in all of it. He is God, and therefore operates within his will and purpose. He is the power that bubbled up in the prophets of the Old Testament and gave them words: 'he spoke through the prophets.' He was present in a unique way in Jesus, from his conception – 'the Holy Spirit will come upon you,' the angel told Mary, 'and the power of the most High will overshadow you' – to his ascension, when, we are told, he received and poured out on his followers 'the promised Holy Spirit'. And the recording of the ways and words of God through the fallible human authors of the Bible was carried out under his motivation and guidance: 'men spoke from God as they were carried along by the Holy Spirit' (2 Peter 1:21).

So the Bible is to be seen as the record of the words and works of God, and especially, for the Christian, of the life and teaching of Jesus. It cannot – or at any rate, should not – be separated from the other ways in which God speaks to us, nor set over against them. But because of its permanence, the written record has a kind of regulative role. Without it, one might say, that pyramid of divine communication would be incoherent.

Yet at the heart of God's communication with us there is the Holy Spirit, not a book. He is the agent of God, making him known in many ways, in many places, through many people. But because he cannot contradict himself, these different revelations stand in an interdependent hierarchy, each depending on the other, each relating to the others, each true within its own terms of reference, and all intended either to interpret or to be interpreted by the written record in the Scriptures.

6 THE BIBLE – INSPIRED, OR INSPIRING?

The idea of a God who 'speaks' – who reveals himself – which is so central to Christianity, has always depended to some degree on the parallel concept of the inspiration of the Scriptures. That is to say, the record of his revelation, whether through history, the prophets, or Jesus, has to be reliable to be of any genuine use to us, and its reliability can only be guaranteed by God himself. After all, no one else knows whether or not it truly represents what he wants to reveal to us – 'those truths which God wishes us to know for our salvation', as the Second Vatican Council put it.

So it is important for Christians to be able to trust the Bible, and it is important also in the task of persuading non-believers of the truth of Christianity. I do not think it is coincidence that the period of the Western Church's most rapid decline – roughly, the period from 1860 to 1960 – coincided with the widespread erosion of the authority and reliability of the Bible, partly as a consequence of Darwinism and partly as a consequence of critical biblical scholarship (largely, one must add, a consequence of the misunderstanding of critical biblical scholarship).

It seems to me that most people now feel unable to return to the unquestioning fundamentalism of past ages, but are nevertheless unsatisfied with an approach to the Bible which treats it as 'just another book', and evacuates it of all authority or reliability. Centuries of Christian experience have told us that this is emphatically *not* 'just another book'. Its impact on human history, its influence in individual human lives and its role in our own spiritual experience as it 'speaks' to us with extraordinary clarity and relevance in our contemporary needs, all endorse its religious authenticity. If God has spoken at all, it seems beyond dispute that he has spoken through these very writings.

But this authenticity of experience – God speaks through the Bible because I hear something – is not an adequate basis for a doctrine of inspiration. It tells me that the Bible is inspiring, but does not prove that it is inspired. Not only that, but it can only speak to and through faith: the non-believer is virtually disqualified from hearing God.

So, is there an *objective* inspiration associated with the Bible? Is there a sense in which it conveys the truth of God (that is, truth *about* God and truth *from* God) quite apart from the disposition of the reader? The orthodox Christian view is that the Holy Spirit inspired – literally, 'breathed into' – the writers, so that what they wrote was guarded from error and accurately revealed the truths of God.

St Paul expresses it in its classic form in his second letter to Timothy:

> All Scripture is God-breathed and is useful for teaching, rebuking, correcting and training in righteousness, so that the man of God may be thoroughly equipped for every good work.[1]

The crucial word in the Greek original is *theopneustos*: 'God-breathed'. All Scripture is 'God-breathed'. The second letter of Peter puts it like this:

> For prophecy never had its origin in the will of man, but men spoke from God as they were carried along by the Holy Spirit.[2]

The 'Scriptures' referred to here are, of course, the Old

Testament: the New Testament was still in process of evolution. But in fact already the letters of Paul are being accorded the status of 'Scripture', as that same second letter of Peter makes clear:

> Bear in mind that our Lord's patience means salvation, just as our dear brother Paul also wrote to you with the wisdom that God gave him. He writes the same way in all his letters, speaking in them of these matters. His letters contain some things that are hard to understand, which ignorant and unstable people distort, as they do the other Scriptures, to their own destruction.[3]

There is no doubt that the apostles — amongst whom the late 'addition' Paul was unquestionably included — were regarded by the early Church as having the same kind of authority as the prophets of the Old Testament. They were in fact seen as speaking with the direct authority of Jesus Christ:

> But the Counsellor, the Holy Spirit, whom the Father will send in my name, will teach you all things and will remind you of everything I have said to you.[4]

From these ideas developed the concept of the inspiration of the Bible, in Old and New Testaments, as a unique, definitive and regulative record of the story of salvation, from creation through the Fall to the calling out of one nation, Israel, and from that to the coming of the promised Redeemer and Saviour and the birth of the 'new' Israel, the Church.

In the nature of things one cannot, of course, prove that a book is inspired by God. That is a matter of faith. But it is possible to find corroborative evidence to support belief, just as it is possible to discover factors that undermine it. Faith, at any rate in its biblical meaning, is not irrational: it does not stand over against evidence, but complements and takes it further, on into realms where human reason cannot arbitrate.

The doctrine of the inspiration of Scripture sits well with the concept of revelation. If God wishes to reveal himself to his creatures, then it is obviously essential that they should have access to a reliable source of that revelation. It is one thing to assert that God speaks; it is quite another to say that he has spoken in a particular way, at a particular place and at a particular time. Yet it is hard to see what value one can put on the statement 'God speaks' or 'God has spoken' if those to whom he speaks are denied access to what he has said, or if the only available reports of what he has said are unreliable, distorted or incorrect.

If, as all Christians believe, Jesus was the ultimate revelation of God to mankind, then it is notable that he treated the Scriptures of the Old Testament as though they spoke the very words of God. He quoted Deuteronomy – 'Man does not live on bread alone, but on every word that comes from the mouth of God' – in the context of using Old Testament Scriptures to refute temptation.[5]

For Jesus, the Scriptures were 'unbreakable': 'the Scripture cannot be broken'. They were the authentic utterance of God, and even he did not have the right to alter them. They had absolute authority.

Yet he regarded his own teachings in the same way. In a Jewish context it was daring to the point of blasphemy that he should put his words on a par with Holy Writ: 'Heaven and earth shall pass away, but my words shall not pass away' (Mark 13:31/Luke 21:33). Consequently, the teaching of Jesus is accorded by Christians the same status as the Old Testament Scriptures (and, in practice, perhaps, a greater one).

However, the teaching of Jesus was oral and spoken words are caught up in the wind and disappear, or lodge for a time in the living memories of people, to die with them. So how could it be that 'my words shall not pass away'?

The answer, I believe, lies in the apostles, the 'special messengers' or 'chosen witnesses', who carried the teaching of Jesus over into the embryonic Church. I have commented already that the writings of the apostles (including Paul) were quickly given the same status as Scripture in the early Church. The reason lies in two factors. Firstly, the apostles brought to the Church a first-hand account (in most cases) of the teaching and actions of Jesus. They were themselves the first preachers of the 'good news' – the *kerygma*, in Greek – the message of salvation encapsulated by Paul in his letter to the Corinthian Church:

> For what I received I passed on to you as of first importance: that Christ died for our sins according to the Scriptures, that he was buried, that he was raised on the third day according to the Scriptures, and that he appeared to Peter, and then to the Twelve. After that, he appeared to more than five hundred of the brothers at the same time, most of whom are still living, though some have fallen asleep. Then he appeared to James, then to all the apostles, and last of all he appeared to me also, as to one abnormally born.[6]

They had, moreover, seen the Lord (the unique apostolic authentication) and had become the recipients of his promise, already quoted from the Fourth Gospel, that the Holy Spirit would keep them from error as they passed on the teaching of Jesus.

So, in a sense, the Christian doctrine of the inspiration of the Bible centres on Jesus and the incarnation, just as one would expect. He endorses the Old Testament, by use and practice; he himself speaks the words of God, which will 'never pass away'; and he authenticates the record of those words, given by the apostles he had chosen. The inspiration of the Bible really depends upon the divine authority of Jesus. If he was 'just another prophet' then this is 'just another book', but if he is the Son of God then here is a uniquely authentic record of what the God who has spoken has said.

Now if this is true, it is true *whether or not the reader believes it*. The doctrine of the inspiration of the Bible, understood in this way, gives it an objective authority. It is true not because I believe it but because God has said it and his Son Jesus has authenticated it. Its authority is the authority of God.

Two difficulties arise at this point. The first is a question. How can I know that the Bible in my hand represents what God has spoken – or even, for that matter, what the prophets or apostles wrote? After all, centuries upon centuries of copying by hand have been known to introduce enormous inaccuracies into ancient manuscripts: it is hard to get even an approximately accurate manuscript of any of Shakespeare's plays, for instance – and compared with Amos, Jeremiah or Ezekiel he is positively modern.

This is a question about the transmission of texts, at one level, and it can be argued out line by line by the experts. Most of them agree that the text of the Old and New Testaments as we now have them are remarkably close to their originals, in so far as one can test the assertion. Certainly the manuscripts of the Old Testament found in the Dead Sea caves nearly forty years ago, which were centuries older than most extant biblical manuscripts, simply prove how the Old Testament we now have is as close as makes no difference to the Old Testament Jesus or John the Baptist would have had.

On another level the question raises a far more fundamental issue. If God has spoken, then part of the deal (if I may put it that way) must be that he keeps the record of what he has said and done free from such errors as would distort its meaning. After all, what use is it to me, in the twentieth century, to know that God inspired a man called Luke to write a Gospel in AD 70 if what I have in my hand is a corruption of what he wrote? Part of any sensible doctrine of the divine inspiration of the Bible must be a parallel divine protection of the text. I believe it has happened, and I believe the proof of it is by your side, or on your bookshelf, as you read this: the ordinary, common or garden Holy Bible you can buy for a pound or two in the High Street.

The second question concerns the concept of truth. If the Bible is inspired by God, then it must be true – indeed, the ultimate truth. Does it follow, then, that every statement the Bible makes (about biology, physics, genetics, history, geography and so on) is part of the truth of God? And – a supplementary – if it *is*, how do we account for factual discrepancies and errors which are demonstrably present in the Bible as we now possess it?

I have dealt with this question at greater length in another book[7], but the answer in a nutshell is that the *purpose* of the revelation defines the scope of the inspiration. The human authors of the Bible were inspired by the Holy Spirit for a specific purpose: to make known to God's human creatures those truths which are necessary for them to find salvation. St Paul defined its purpose in his first letter to Timothy – a crucial passage which I have already quoted in a different context:

> All Scripture is God-breathed and is useful for teaching, rebuking, correcting and training in righteousness.

There is no word here of divinely inspired information about biology, history or science, except, of course, insofar as they touch on the stated objects. History, for example, is important when it is the raw material of God's activity in salvation: the incarnation, the crucifixion and the resurrection occurred within human history, and reliable information about them is essential if we are to know what God wants to say to us. But no issues of salvation and no truths of God are at stake in the identification of obscure high priests, provincial governors or ancient cities.

It is also important to say that what the Bible deals with all through is the truth of God, rather than factual information. So much of the truth of the Bible lies in metaphor, imagery, symbol and poetry that the very question 'Is it true?' demands first of all that we establish what *kind* of truth the author is offering us. It is a peculiarly modern obsession to elevate accurate factual reporting ('Just tell me the facts') above the most profound but symbolic or allegorical truth. The Bible deals in both, but it is important to know which kind of truth we are dealing with before we strike attitudes about the reliability or inerrancy of the Scriptures.

For me, as I think for many Christians today, it is sufficient that the Bible tells me the truth of God: truth *about* God, *from* God. The literary forms in which it is couched, and the precise intentions of the original writer, are important if I am to understand it correctly, but the really vital thing is to hear and receive the truth in whatever form it comes to *me*. Leslie Newbiggin has made this point most effectively in a recent book:

> In what way does Scripture function as the bearer of revelation? I have emphasised its variety, and it goes without saying that modern scholarship has brought to light an immensely complex network of different strands within each of these elements. It has uncovered the many different sources from which material has been drawn, and the social, cultural, religious, political and economic interests which have played a part in shaping it. Yet the bible comes to us in its 'canonical shape', the result of many centuries of interpretation and re-interpretation, editing and re-editing, with a unity which depends upon certain discernible centres. These are events, happenings in the contingent world of history, which are interpreted as disclosures in a unique sense of the presence and action of God. Essentially there are two primary centres – the rescue of Israel from Egypt, and the events concerning the man Jesus of Nazareth.[8]

For me, this approach helps to resolve the rather pointless

argument about historicity: did the whale *really* swallow
Jonah, or did Jesus *really* turn water into wine? Our best
attempts at scholarly analysis, at comparative textual study,
at stripping away this and that layer of cultural conditioning,
may in the end simply blind us to the truth that God has put
there, which jumps out at the ordinary, believing reader
without any recourse to such academic examination. In these
examples, for instance, who can doubt that the *truth* about
Jonah is that those whom God calls to carry his message
cannot close their ears to that vocation? At whatever cost, to
whatever lengths, the 'Hound of Heaven' will pursue them
until they respond. The whale is not a bad picture of the
will of God! And one can argue that the *truth* behind
Cana of Galilee is that Jesus came to turn the insipid
water of a legalistic religion into the rich, reviving wine of
the kingdom of heaven. He who, in the language of the
Fourth Gospel, was the agent of creation, the source of life
and light, could take the basic elements of our survival —
wine, here, and bread, later — and make them means of
grace.

Now those truths are truths of God, truths in the spiritual
realm. They leave unanswered questions which our pedantic
and inquisitive minds nag away at: 'Was there a whale?' 'Was
it real wine?' Human wisdom will come up with this and that
answer (for me, in these two cases, 'no' and 'yes', respective-
ly), but divine wisdom refuses to be categorised. I am not
saying that divine truth is divorced from factual truth, but
that it is greater than it. When we have done our best to
understand what the original authors intended, and translated their words as faithfully and reliably as we can, we still
fall short unless the Spirit of God, the ultimate author, makes
known the thoughts of God, those 'spiritual truths in spiritual words' which St Paul spoke of to his friends in Corinth.
That truth, which 'God has revealed to us by his Spirit', is
'God's secret wisdom', 'the deep things of God', the very
'thoughts of God'.[9]

Beside that truth, that wisdom, those thoughts, all our

scholarship and all our arguing begin to look a trifle inadequate. But that may be the very moment when true understanding begins.

7 JESUS OF NAZARETH: THE KEY?

A few miles off the Italian coast, opposite Naples and Vesuvius, lies the beautiful island of Capri, an exquisite playground for the rich Europeans and Americans of today. At one end of the island, towering above the vine-groves, the sun-drenched white houses and the rocky headland, stand the remains of the palace of Tiberius Caesar. The ruins in their splendour look down on the uncannily blue sea of Capri, hundreds of feet below at the foot of precipitous cliffs. From this island fortress Tiberius ruled the entire Roman Empire for the last few years of his life, from about AD 28 to AD 37. Under his command the legions of Rome maintained the *pax Romana* – a 'peace through strength' if there ever was one – from what is today Russia to the deserts of North Africa.

Among the smaller provinces to 'enjoy' the civilising benefits of Roman rule was Judaea, some 1200 miles or so from the Emperor's palace on Capri. While he drank wine there, and undoubtedly hunted the wild boar for which the island was famous, a religious leader was emerging in that tiny Province whose fame and influence would eventually infinitely outshine his own. Today not many people beyond professional historians could tell you much about Tiberius Caesar, but a third of the world's population know the name of the Roman proconsul who authorised this prophet's execution, and even more the name of the prophet himself. Jesus of Nazareth, the prophet from Galilee, has guaranteed

Pontius Pilatus a notoriety he could well have done without, while the great Emperor himself, regarded as divine by many of his followers, is probably best known today as a mere footnote in the story of Jesus, whose baptism at the hands of John the Baptist occurred, Luke tells us, 'in the fifteenth year of the reign of Tiberius Caesar' – AD 29.

It may seem far-fetched to suggest that a penniless preacher from a rural backwater of the Roman Empire offers us the key to the understanding of the purposes of God in human history. It may seem even more incredible to claim that he was and is the divine Son of God, the ultimate revelation to his creatures. Yet millions of apparently sane and intelligent people today do make those claims, as did his first followers. The Fourth Gospel, undoubtedly the work of an eye-witness of the ministry of Jesus, records the claim, 'I am the way, the truth and the life. No one comes to the Father except through me' (John 14:6). Whether these are the actual words of Jesus, or a subsequent recollection of ideas he expressed to his followers, they represent a quite staggering claim. In essence, they propose that Jesus himself is the key with which we may unlock the purpose ('the way'), the truth and the power ('the life') of God.

That is the claim which I wish to examine in this section of the book: that God has spoken, and what he has said is best, most clearly and most completely expressed in Jesus, his Son. As the Epistle to the Hebrews puts it, 'God, who gave to our forefathers many different glimpses of the truth, has now . . . given us the truth in his Son' (Hebrews 1:1).

If God exists, and if he has communicated with his creatures, Jesus is important, if only because so many people claim to have found in him the clue, the necessary key, to that communication. That is why I am now turning to consider the third area of Christian belief, the place of Jesus in the scheme of things. Perhaps because he *is* seen as the 'key' by so many, he is also seen as the focal point of attack by many of Christianity's critics. Already, for instance, I have called him as evidence both for the nature of God – especially as a God who 'speaks' in an interpersonal relationship with human beings – and for the divine authentication of the Scriptures. Now we have to ask, can this one figure of history, however influential he may have proved to be, really be seen as the incarnate Son of God, his final and ultimate 'word' to the human race? Or is this, as some have claimed, a piece of wishful thinking on a cosmic scale, and a gross distortion of the historical evidence?

In an earlier book[1], already quoted, I have looked at that historical evidence and tried to suggest an outline of the life of Jesus that is consistent with it. I do not propose to go over that ground again, but rather to look at the main objections to it – the case *against* the divinity of Jesus, as it were – to see whether the sceptics and the critics have really made the kind of case that renders the traditional belief in him as the Son of God quite untenable. If they have, then that has repercussions on much that has gone before in this book, especially in the area of the authority of the Bible. If their case against his divinity is unconvincing we will find, as in the debate over creation, a century of scholarly criticism beginning to melt away before the evidence, like the Arctic ice-cap in the Spring. Then the 'key' will be a valid one, which we may legitimately use to open a whole treasure-store of knowledge about ourselves, God, and his purpose for us.

The most persistent attack on the historical credentials of Jesus, or at any rate on the Gospel records of his life, has probably come from the demythologisers. These were the critics who started from the premise that the Gospels were overlaid with accretions – ideas that had little to do with Jesus of Nazareth but a great deal to do with the way Christianity developed in the Graeco-Roman world. Somewhere underneath the layers of myth, if only one could strip them off, it might be possible to find the 'real' Jesus, but the task was a daunting one. Indeed, the great German theologian Rudolf Bultmann eventually came to the conclusion that it was virtually impossible to know anything for certain about the historical Jesus, so complex and confusing are the layers of myth which have wound themselves around and even penetrated into the heart of the historical material. For him, it was pointless looking for the life or teaching of the historical Jesus in the Gospels, because their compilers simply were not interested in it. They were only concerned to put across the ideas of the emerging Christian religion in the form of these stories.

Not all scholars, by a long way, went as far as that and more recently the emphasis has shifted away from demythologising to an examination of the Gospel records in the light of the Judaism of the time. However, the idea that the Gospels consist of a small core of historical material surrounded and penetrated by mythological accretions has taken root in the popular mind. Without being fully articulated, it undoubtedly shapes the way many modern people approach the Gospels. They feel free to pick and choose the parts they like and do not like, to disregard (if they wish) the supernatural element in the Gospels and to regard Jesus as the one thing the Gospels simply will not allow him to be seen as – a great and gifted religious teacher who made no pretensions to be anything more than that. In some extreme cases people have felt they have the freedom to rewrite the Gospel material to present a different 'Christ': not the Jesus of history but the Christ of human experience, a kind of cosmic projection of human ideals, revolutionary fervour, or mystic experiences. Indeed, many theologians in the Bultmann tradition would say that all we can be sure of today is our own faith-experience, arising out of the community of faith, the Church, which – in its better moments – will pick up and transmit the faith-experience of those who have gone before, right back to the so-called 'Christ event'.

The process by which the 'demythologisers' reached these conclusions is an interesting one. It undoubtedly began with an extreme scepticism about anything miraculous or supernatural. If you have decided, as an *a priori* assumption, that nothing happens, or has ever happened, which is contrary to the so-called rules of nature, then of course it also follows that

Jesus did not do miracles, was not 'divine' and did not rise from the dead.

The next, or maybe even parallel, development was the growth of 'higher criticism' – the study of the Bible, and in this case particularly the New Testament, as though it were not only an 'ordinary' book (which in one sense it is) but a highly suspect one, the product of quite a long period of evolution during the first centuries of church history, heavily influenced by the ideas of the surrounding Graeco-Roman culture. Higher criticism and religious scepticism are blood-brothers, and the one can fuel the other. Scholars who do not like the supernatural element in the New Testament can quickly slip into dubbing it the mythical element, and it then becomes a necessary exercise to try to remove this mythical element in order to get at the bare bones of the Jesus story.

However, the awkward fact is that it simply does not work. When the textual scholars have completed their task, separating the very earliest and most 'primitive' elements in the Gospels from the rest, what do we find? There, right in the heart of what is universally recognised as the 'core' material about Jesus, is that very 'supernatural' element. Far from being added later, it is there right from the start, as many radical scholars have recognised. The miracles of Jesus are as much a part of any historical backbone to the Gospel as are his parables.

But the case goes further than that. In AD 54, the apostle Paul wrote to the church at Corinth, which he had helped to found a few years earlier. In the course of this letter, which is one of the earliest documents of the New Testament, he reminds them of what he preached to them. But, he says, he delivered to them 'what I also received'. In other words, the message he gave them at the time of their conversion to Christianity was the one he was given at the time of his own conversion, some twenty years earlier.

That takes us back almost to the time of Jesus himself, certainly to within two or three years of his crucifixion. The implications of this for our evaluation of the New Testament are irresistible. For what Paul lists as the essence of that early message, from the earliest days of the Church, is that 'Christ died for our sins . . . was buried, and that he was raised on the third day'. In other words, the miracle of the resurrection, the single central miracle of the New Testament, is shown to be not a later accretion but part of the very message that brought Christianity into being.

The truth is that whichever allegedly mythical element we take in the synoptic Gospels (Matthew, Mark and Luke), if we trace it back by the soundest methods of textual scholarship we shall find its roots in the earliest sources. Indeed, so strong is this evidence that most scholars now, including some of the greatest sceptics, will agree that the miracles of Jesus – of healing and exorcism – are part of the historical record of his life. We may not interpret the events as his contemporaries did, but that he was known as a healer and exorcist of quite extraordinary charisma is as good as proven.

It is hard to take seriously, in the light of all this, the argument that the Gospel writers were not interested in recording history about Jesus. Why, otherwise, should they choose *biography* as their preferred medium? Why should they have included stories, incidents and sayings which appear to conflict with, or at any rate raise difficult questions about, the teaching of that emerging Christian religion? (see Matthew 10:5-6, Luke 9:27). It is a Jewish, not a Christian, historian who has said of this argument: 'Bultmann's dictum about the impossibility of knowing anything about Jesus or his personality "because the early Christian sources show no interest in either", becomes a plain misjudgment.'[2]

That brings us to the second common objection: that the idea of Jesus as the divine Son of God is a later invention, only really incorporated into Christianity after the Council of Chalcedon in AD 451. Later ages, it is said, have misunderstood the meaning of the Gospel references to Jesus as the Son of God, reading into them later ideas about a 'double nature' and incarnate divinity which would have been totally foreign not only to the Gospel writers, but also to the beliefs of Jesus himself.

In popular thought, St Paul is the villain in all this. It was he, they say, who took the simple message of the Jesus of the earlier Gospels, the Synoptics, and complicated it with his ideas of a divine Being 'in the form of God', the 'fullness of the godhead in bodily form'. The *real* Jesus, in this scenario, was a straightforward, uncomplicated rabbi with an eye for a good story and a powerful moral, who would be astonished to find that today millions worship him as the Son of the God.

Once again, the theory does not stand up to serious examination. At the most basic level, most of the letters of St Paul, which are said to complicate the simple Gospel narratives, were written *before* the Gospels. The compilers of the Gospels would undoubtedly have been familiar with Paul's epistles, have agreed with their theology, and have understood it to be the application, in terms of salvation and church life, of the message and works of Jesus which they record. The Gospels were written in churches planted by men like Paul, preaching the same message. They were intended to preserve for later generations a reliable record of the words and actions of Jesus, before the oral tradition which had passed on that record for the first three decades of the Church's history became distorted or corrupted. The Gospels stand alongside the letters of Paul and Peter, complementing them and providing the evidence about Jesus upon which the apostles based their case. The idea of a conflict between the Gospels and the Epistles is a modern invention, as is the notion of a 'simple' Jesus and a 'complicated' Paul. Jesus is not nearly as 'simple' as most people think, and Paul's complexity is more to do with his methodology than his message. Paul believed Jesus to be the incarnate Son of God, before whom one day every knee should bow. I do not believe Mark or Luke – both close associates of Paul over many years – would have dissented in the smallest particular from his beliefs about Jesus.

A rather different objection, though arriving at much the

same conclusion as the demythologisers, is that a serious distortion of the original (and very Jewish) understanding of Jesus occurred as the Church moved out of the Jewish world and into the Greek one. It is a case very persuasively argued by a distinguished Jewish scholar, Geza Vermes, of Oxford University. He sees Jesus as an incomparably gifted prophet – 'second to none in profundity of insight and grandeur of character'. He even goes as far as to agree that he was 'venerated by his intimates and less committed admirers alike as prophet, Lord and son of God'.[3]

But Vermes regards these statements, taken within the context of first-century Judaism, as falling far short of the interpretation later put upon them by the Christian Church. For him, Jesus was a charismatic prophet of a kind common enough in that time (though incomparably superior to the rest), 'lord' in the sense of a man to be revered and respected, and 'son of God' in the way the phrase is used in the writings of Judaism to refer to a man of God, a descendant of David and (possibly) the Messiah. But Jesus was not, he argues, regarded by his Jewish contemporaries – not even by his disciples – as a being with two natures, human and divine, nor as the incarnate and divine Son of God as Christians later saw him.

Vermes believes that what happened was that these symbolic and colourful titles bestowed upon a teacher and prophet of the undoubted gifts and holiness of Jesus within contemporary Judaism were *misunderstood* by the Greek converts to Christianity. As the Greek element grew in the Church, and the Hebrew element dwindled, so ideas far removed from the intentions of those who first applied the titles to Jesus became common, and were finally incorporated into the creeds of the Church.

That is his theory, and, as I have said, it is persuasively argued. But again, I feel, it simply does not stand up. No one in the New Testament – indeed, hardly anyone in the entire history of the Church – has used more extravagant language about Jesus than St Paul. For him, Jesus shares the nature of

God – he was 'in the form (*en morphe*, in Greek) of God'. In him 'the fullness of the Deity lives in bodily form' (Colossians 2:9). Before him every knee shall bow (see Philippians 2:6–10). No impartial reader of Paul's letters could doubt that he regarded Jesus as divine, though also fully human, and that when he called him the Son of God he meant substantially what the Christians of the succeeding centuries meant when they said it.

But Paul was Hebrew, not Greek! He was, in his own words, 'a Hebrew of the Hebrews', 'a Pharisee, the son of a Pharisee' (Philippians 3:5, Acts 23:6). Can it seriously be suggested that the converted rabbi, steeped in the Judaism of his day, misunderstood the titles ascribed to Jesus by his own Jewish contemporaries? Paul's conversion occurred in the very early years of the Church, *before* Christianity moved out into the Greek world. Indeed, he was to become himself the chief instrument of that expansion. His understanding of the nature of Jesus was not, so far as we know, challenged by the other apostles. On the contrary, his ministry was warmly endorsed by the first Council of the Church, at Jerusalem.

The real difficulty lies, in my view, elsewhere. Anyone who studies the Gospels closely, as Vermes has done, is bound to be impressed with the spiritual calibre of Jesus. In a book published in Hebrew fifty years ago, another Jewish scholar, Joseph Klausner, wrote of Jesus: 'In his ethical code there is a sublimity, distinctiveness and originality in form unparalleled in any other Hebrew ethical code.'[4] Vermes himself has written, 'No objective and enlightened student of the Gospels can help but be struck by the incomparable superiority of Jesus . . . second to none in profundity of insight and grandeur of character.'

This holy and good man, whom every reader of the Gospels admires, is regarded by Christians as the divine Son of God. Indeed, they believe he claimed to be no less, though careful Christians will concede that he never actually claimed it in so many words. So non-Christian admirers are driven to argue that there is a vast gulf between Jesus and the Church's beliefs about him. They do not want to denigrate Jesus, but they do want to reject the Christian's belief in him as divine.

So the argument really comes down to this. Did Jesus *himself* believe he was the divine Son of God? Obviously Klausner and Vermes do not think he did, and neither, for rather different reasons, do the demythologisers. Undoubtedly the 'orthodox' case has at times been overstated, or based on too glib and conditioned a view of the New Testament material. Yet I believe that the evidence is there – and, again, in the 'core' material – to show that Jesus did indeed see himself as related to God the Father in a unique way.

Let us take first of all one of the absolutely definitive statements of Jesus, recorded by Matthew and Luke, on the subject of exorcisms. The Jewish religious establishment was obviously worried by the way in which Jesus was successful in exorcising people who were (in the language of the day) 'possessed by evil spirits'. The contemporary view of this was that such people had been invaded by a devil or devils, agents of Satan, the adversary. Exorcisms were indeed practised by other charismatic prophets, but it would seem that Jesus was different, firstly, in the scale and success of his exorcisms, and secondly in their form: he cast out devils on his own authority.

On this occasion the Jewish lawyers made the suggestion that in fact what Jesus was doing was casting out lesser devils by invoking the prince of devils, Beelzebub (see Matthew 12:22-28, Luke 11:14-20). This accusation would damage Jesus in two ways: it would, if true, discredit him as a man of God, and it would also undermine the favourable impression which his authoritative style had made on the crowds. 'The people were amazed, because he spoke as one who had authority, and not like the scribes' – but if that authority were in fact satanic what they had until now seen as commendable would be rejected as totally opposed to the ways of God.

Jesus countered this accusation trenchantly. He ridiculed

the very idea of one of Satan's princes being used (by him or by anybody else) to counter Satan's work. That would indeed be 'a house divided against itself', he argued. Having dismissed the charge, he then turned it against his detractors. 'But if I drive out demons by the finger of God,' he said, 'then the kingdom of God has come to you.' His use of the phrase 'finger of God' (a Hebraism translated literally into Greek) is very significant, though it is hard to convey its full significance in English. Perhaps 'If I, *using the very power of God himself*, cast out devils' gets near it. Matthew has, 'If I by the Spirit of God . . .' It is beyond doubt a claim to divine authority, paralleling the charge that he had used the power of the prince of devils. Far from it, he asserts: indeed, quite the contrary. I have used the power of God himself.

Let us next consider the way in which Jesus took it upon himself to forgive sins. A notable example is in the story of the healing of the paralysed man who was lowered down through the roof of a house into the room where Jesus was healing the sick. Confronted by this helpless cripple, Jesus simply said, 'Son, your sins are forgiven' – a reply which led the watching teachers of the law to say to themselves, 'Why does this fellow talk like that? He's blaspheming! Who can forgive sins but God alone?'

Now this alleged comment (and it can only be 'alleged' because it was what they were 'thinking to themselves') might be dismissed as editorial comment by the Gospel-writer but for what followed it. For Jesus 'knowing in his Spirit what they were thinking in their hearts', addressed a question to the bystanders:

'Why are you thinking these things? Which is easier: to say to the paralytic, "Your sins are forgiven" or to say, "Get up, take your mat and walk"? But that you may know that the Son of Man has authority on earth to forgive sins . . .' He said to the paralytic, 'I tell you get up, take your mat and go home.' He got up, took his mat and walked out in full view of them all. This amazed everyone and they praised God, saying, 'We have never seen anything like this!'[5]

Clearly the claim by Jesus that he has 'authority on earth to forgive sins' was exceptional, to say the least, if the response of the onlookers was that they had 'never seen anything like this!'

That is important because Vermes argues that it was not unheard of for prophets and other religious leaders in Judaism to pronounce people's sins to be forgiven. He gives a few instances in the book already quoted. But in fact none of them is as bold and decisive as the words of Jesus, 'Your sins are forgiven.' It was presumably that boldness that amazed the crowd, as also the fact that he explicitly took on the charge of blasphemy and turned it against his accusers, not by denying that he forgave sins but by proving that he had authority to do so.

Thirdly, let us consider a strange saying of Jesus, in which he himself asked the Jews, 'What do you think about the Messiah? Whose son is he?'[6]

'The son of David' they replied.

Jesus responded in a typically Jewish way, by asking another question. 'How is it then that David, speaking by the Spirit, calls him "Lord"? For he says, "The Lord said to my Lord: Sit at my right hand, until I put your enemies under your feet." If then David calls him "Lord", how can he be his son?' Matthew comments that 'no one could say a word in reply'.

The Old Testament text quoted by Jesus, from Psalm 110, was to become a favourite of the early Church. Indeed, Luke reports it from the lips of Peter on the day of Pentecost, as the climax, the clinching piece of evidence, in his argument that 'God has made this Jesus, whom you crucified, both Lord and Messiah'. But here it is being used by Jesus himself, in a passage in the synoptic Gospels of undoubted authenticity, in his own distinctive style and idiom of teaching, to argue a similar case: that he is not simply 'the son of David' (a messianic title) but David's 'Lord'.

It would be going too far to say that this established beyond doubt that Jesus claimed divinity, but it certainly proves that he regarded himself as 'greater' (in rank and status) than the great king of Israel from whose line the Messiah would come, and by the use of that particular text from the Psalms came very close indeed to claiming a unique relationship to Yahweh: 'The Lord (Yahweh) said to my Lord (Jesus), sit at my right hand.' The verse is certainly messianic, but the way Jesus applies it goes far beyond the usual messianic language. He is David's *Lord*.

I think that the evidence that Jesus believed himself to be the unique representative of God on earth is overwhelming. It is not to be based simply on the usual proof texts, most of them found in the Fourth Gospel and therefore the objects of scholarly scepticism, on the grounds that they are not verbatim records of the words of Jesus, but John's interpretation of them. It is to be found in every layer of the Gospel material and, as we have seen, as much in what Jesus did as what he said. It is so deeply embedded and so integral that the casual reader may miss it, and yet it does not require specialist knowledge to recognise it. After all, millions of ordinary Christians reading the New Testament down the centuries have had little difficulty in seeing there a portrait of one who was both human and divine, son of Man and Son of God.

It may well be asked why it is so important to decide whether Jesus was, and believed himself to be, the Son of God on earth. The reason is absolutely central to the whole argument of this book, and indeed to the whole Christian case. Bishop Stephen Neill has expressed it pungently in a recent book.

For many generations Christians have been accustomed to listen on Christmas day to the reading of the prologue to the Gospel of St John, and many have been puzzled by the opening phrase: 'In the beginning was the Word.' Who is this Word, and what has he to do with Jesus Christ? If for the mysterious 'logos' we read 'revelation', things become much clearer; this great passage deals with a God who desires to make himself known, and in particular wants to make himself known to the human race.[7]

As we have already seen, God has 'made himself known' in many different ways, of different degrees of clarity and intensity: through the order and beauty of creation; through conscience and our moral questionings; through the prophets of Israel, culminating in the astonishing figure of John the Baptist. But 'in these last days', as Stephen Neill continues, 'he has spoken to us through his Son.'

And then this revealing God once for all took three-dimensional form, in which human beings might recognise their own true nature, and so recognise the Word of God: 'the Word' became one of us and lived a human life like ours.[8]

The heart of God's communication, of the whole idea of God as 'communicator', in fact, is in this principle of 'incarnation'. It is fraught with possible misunderstandings, of course, but in the concept of God taking 'three dimensional form' (in Stephen Neill's daring phrase) there is a fundamental truth that anyone can grasp.

Most of the great world religions start from much the same point: that 'God' is good – indeed, morally perfect – and that mankind is not. This creates a gulf between humanity and divinity which must somehow be bridged, so that human beings can be restored to a good relationship with God. I fully realise that Buddhists or Hindus, for instance, might not recognise in that language anything remotely like their religion. And yet I believe it is true (given the variety of divine names and the various ways in which the idea of 'sin' is expressed) that they too postulate a world in which people need to move upwards, towards God or Ultimate Being and out of the darkness and depravity of our corrupted world.

The different religions offer different means towards attaining this. For some, the answer lies in obedience to law, rule and ritual. For others, it is in offerings and sacrifices. For others, it is in a combination of the 'good life' and 'good thoughts', making it possible for us to be caught up and up into the Eternal. Great prophets and teachers have shown the way, but it is left to us, within the support systems of religious beliefs and practices, to attain holiness and union with God. In other words, and to over-simplify, the universal religious answer to the question 'How can I be right with God?' is 'Do what he requires'. By whatever means he demands, it is our responsibility to attain the goal.

Christianity – alone, I think, of world religions – reverses the priorities. God is good – indeed, perfect. We are flawed – indeed, 'sinners'. We cannot come to God, *so God comes to us*. The incarnation says that God took the initiative in communication and 'came among us'.

> *He came down to earth from heaven*
> *Who is God and Lord of all,*
> *And his shelter was a stable*
> *And his cradle was a stall . . .*

Fanny Alexander had an uncanny way of putting complex ideas with devastating simplicity in her hymns, and this is no exception. However, there are dangers in expressing things vividly, and there is no doubt that hymns like this one, and church language down the centuries, have sometimes given people the impression that between 2 BC and AD 33 (or whatever the precise dates were) heaven was empty and the universe leaderless while God took a trip to Palestine. To say that the baby Jesus was divine, for instance, is not to concur with the view that the totality of divinity was encompassed by those seven or eight pounds of flesh and blood wrapped in swaddling clothes and lying in a manger. 'God was in Christ', in St Paul's words, but the Creator still sustained the creation and his Spirit still moved restlessly to and fro in the Universe about his purposes. To say 'Jesus is God' (which is more than, though not against, what the Bible says) is not the same as saying 'God is Jesus', whatever the rules of grammar say.

After all, for thirty-six hours or so, from Good Friday evening until Easter morning, Jesus was dead. But God, by definition, cannot die. He still maintained his role as the architect, creator and sustainer of all that is, even while his Son's body lay lifeless in a tomb. The incarnation is an amazing, daring concept: the ultimate in communication. But it is distorted if it is represented, even incidentally, as a matter of 'God coming down to earth', for all the world like the ludicrous gods of Greece and Rome at sport with their bewildered creatures. God was present in Jesus, yes. But best of all God perfectly *expressed himself* in Jesus. He was the 'Word of God', God's self-revelation. That is why, in the memorable sentence of the Fourth Gospel, Jesus can say, 'Anyone who has seen me has seen the Father' (John 14:9). Or, in the even more remarkable words – more remarkable because they are in the heart of the synoptic material in Matthew's Gospel – 'No one knows the Son except the Father, and no one knows the Father except the Son and those to whom the Son chooses to reveal him' (Matthew 11:27).

There is an instance of perfect communication, on a person-to-person level. The Father communicates perfectly with the Son, so that they have perfect knowledge of each other. And the Son communicates that knowledge perfectly to 'those to whom he chooses to reveal' it. Here at last the Great Communicator achieves his purpose: the possibility that human beings may have access to unflawed, undistorted, totally reliable knowledge of himself. This is much, much more than a temporary, dazzling appearance of God on earth. This is God revealing himself *to* humans *through* a human. That is why Christians have always fought – not always completely successfully – to maintain the true humanity as well as the real divinity of Jesus. They can see enough of themselves in Jesus to recognise their own nature; and they can see enough of God in him to discover 'the way, the truth and the life'.

The cross is in many ways the culmination of this discovery. If Jesus came to show us what God is like and – in the manner of Moses – deliver us from evil, then his death said it all. Here was God's identification with us in our plight carried to the ultimate: 'God so loved the world that he gave his only Son, that whoever believes in him shall not perish but have eternal life' (John 3:16). In Jesus, God not only entered human nature, but experienced its most bitter element, death.

There seems little doubt that Jesus saw his role as Messiah not simply in the rather triumphalist terms of the Deliverer ('one like Moses') but also as the Suffering Servant of Yahweh, prophesied by Isaiah. He did not come to *show* us the way to God, but to *be* the way; and he did that by offering himself as a sacrifice, dying (as the New Testament sees it) 'for us', as some eternal reparation for all the centuries of human disobedience, injustice and sin. He delivered us, in other words, not by conquest but by redemption – by paying the price of our freedom. No one can expect to plumb the mystery of the cross, but somewhere at its heart is the image of perfect self-denial delivering the human race from the awful consequences of self-assertion.

The final demonstration of the divinity of Jesus, and the seal on the authenticity of the revelation he gave us, is undoubtedly the resurrection. That probably accounts for the persistence of the attack on its objective reality in recent decades. If Jesus were 'merely' a prophet, no matter how holy, how eloquent and how influential, then death was his end. That he died, 'crucified under Pontius Pilate', is one of the best-attested facts about him.

But if, as his followers claimed, he rose from the dead – was seen by them, re-commissioned them, sent them out to proclaim his message to the whole world – then this was no ordinary prophet. In the words of the apostle Paul, some twenty or so years after the event, 'Jesus . . . as to his human nature was a descendant of David' but 'through the Spirit of holiness was declared with power to be the Son of God by his resurrection from the dead' (Romans 1:3-4).

So powerful is the evidence in the New Testament and beyond it of the transformation of the disciples after the crucifixion, and so obviously sincere their belief in the resurrection, that few biblical or historical scholars choose to refute it head-on. There really is no doubt at all that the first Christians believed that Jesus had returned to them and was 'alive' again in every normal sense of the word. The apostles put it most simply: 'We have seen the Lord.' That was their unanimous testimony, and they maintained it in the face of ridicule, persecution, torture and execution. It would take some plot, some hallucination, some 'inner psychological experience', to produce so uniform, coherent and convinced a testimony. It seems indisputable that an objective event, of a totally unexpected, surprising and inexplicable nature, brought about this transformation of the disciples. That is their own explanation, and it is hard to find a credible alternative.

Nevertheless, such is the implacable hostility of the modern mind to anything that cannot be explained in terms of our science and our understanding of existence, many people have spent a great deal of effort trying to find an alternative explanation.

Fundamentally, these alternatives break down into two distinct groups. On the one hand, there are those who say that the disciples were mistaken (genuinely, but completely) in their understanding of what had happened. The accounts in the Gospels are contradictory, the alleged events confusing and confused, and the interpretation put on them is wrong. The details behind this case vary. Sometimes the disciples were the victims of someone else's plot (to steal his body and then proclaim that the prophet Jesus had come back from the dead, for instance). Sometimes they reported what they saw but interpreted it wrongly – Jesus did not die on the cross, but was in a coma from which he revived in the cold tomb, and from whence (in the most extreme versions) he escaped, making off with Mary of Magdala to the South of France and starting a family. Sometimes it is suggested that the disciples went to the wrong tomb, and jumped to all sorts of wrong conclusions when they found it empty. And sometimes, at perhaps the other end of rationality, the whole thing is seen as an elaborate spiritualist seance, with Jesus appearing in spirit form from 'the other side' to his bewildered disciples – who, once again, completely misinterpreted this gesture.

The second group of explanations are more sophisticated, and rather harder to refute. The details again may vary, but the heart of the argument is that the resurrection was not an objective event – it is often said that the remains of Jesus lie somewhere in Palestine – but a spiritual experience on the part of the disciples, which they later explained in pictorial terms. It was the early Church that misunderstood, in this version, taking stories that were meant to illustrate the enormous, transforming experience of Jesus which the disciples had after his death to be factual accounts of something that actually happened.

Both of these are interesting examples of communication problems! But they are also instances of an almost perverse refusal to take the Gospels seriously as history. Of course it is *interpreted* history – its authors all believed in the resurrection of Jesus, and filtered their accounts of him through that belief. But *all* history is interpreted: it comes to us through the records of men and women who had views, beliefs, prejudices about what they were reporting. But that does not make us automatically assume that there is no historical basis to their accounts. We simply learn to 'aim off', to allow for the views (and prejudices, where necessary) of the reporters.

Happily we are no longer in a theological climate in which – for a great many distinguished scholars – the search for an historical Jesus was an illusion. But there remains this vestigial suspicion of the Gospels – especially the Fourth –

and a widespread disinclination to treat them with the seriousness they deserve. Almost any daft theory, no matter how flimsily based or historically unlikely, can be guaranteed a hearing – and even a television documentary. Meanwhile, the Gospel accounts, which careful scholarship has demonstrated to be valuable historical documents, are often treated in a cavalier way, as though the eye-witnesses were perjured or deluded.

For instance, in that first group of explanations, even a cursory examination of the Gospels shows that most of them are unconvincing. If the body was stolen – by friend or foe – why on earth would they leave behind its linen wrappings, as evidence of the deed? And yet the Gospel accounts record, in passing, the presence of the burial cloths in the tomb. If the disciples went to the wrong tomb, and then mistakenly proclaimed that Jesus had risen from the dead, why did not their opponents – who were numerous and influential – open up the *real* tomb, exhume the body of Jesus and demolish the new Jesus movement at birth? And as for the notion that Jesus did not die on the cross, it can only be said that no forensic scientist would support it. Crucifixion was irreversibly fatal from quite soon after the victim was hung on the cross, from dislocation of joints and rupture of internal organs. Certainly no one who had been on a cross for an hour or more would ever walk again, let alone raise a family. The spiritualist argument, too, founders on the Gospel records. Jesus is actually reported as denying that he was a 'spirit', presumably in order to scotch any notion that his resurrection was not objectively real (Luke 24:37ff).

With regard to the second group of arguments, the case is different, of course. Those who take this line are not only arguing that Jesus did not rise from the dead – in any normal meaning of those words – but that the Gospels do not mean what they appear to say or, perhaps, do not say what they appear to mean. The Gospel 'evidence' is accepted (at one level) but interpreted in an illustrative or parabolic way. 'This,' the disciples are imagined as saying, 'is what the resurrection experience was like. It was *as though* Jesus stood among us, broke bread with us, joined us on the seashore, recommissioned us as his special messengers.' So when they say they 'saw the Lord' this is interpreted as meaning that they 'encountered' him in a new way, had a fresh and powerful experience of him, 'saw' new truth about him – especially about his crucifixion. This, the argument goes, was the Easter event – the return of *faith* to the disciples on a massive scale.

It is an interesting argument, and I have spent many happy hours debating it with some of its most eloquent advocates. But I am always left where I began. *This is not what the first Christians have told us.* This is a modern reinterpretation of an essentially simple narrative: in my view, it reads into it what is not there, in order to remove from it an element which is unacceptable to some modern minds – the miraculous.

I am not saying that there are no 'problems' in the Gospel accounts of the resurrection. There manifestly are contradictions of detail, and some points where the different sources (the oral traditions, the resurrection stories collected in different centres of the early Church, and the reminiscences of the eye-witness of the Fourth Gospel) are difficult, if not impossible to reconcile. What comes through to the unprejudiced reader, however, is one absolutely unanimous piece of testimony: 'We have seen the Lord.' One might add to that, 'And his tomb was empty.'

This testimony is not a later development or refinement; it is there in the earliest records. When the apostle Paul wrote to the Church at Corinth in AD 54 – a mere twenty years after the crucifixion – he gave a bald, factual account of the resurrection as the substance of the gospel he had preached to them a couple of years earlier: 'Christ died for our sins according to the Scriptures . . . was buried . . . raised on the third day . . . and appeared to Peter and then to the Twelve' (1 Corinthians 15:3-5).

Not only that, but this message which he had preached to them was one which, he said, he had himself 'received . . . as

of first importance'. In other words, it was the gospel he had
believed at his own conversion, which takes us back almost to
the time of the first Easter – certainly within a few years.
That is not much time for a mythical structure to develop!

The truth is often stranger than fiction. In this case it is
also more convincing. There simply was not time between
the events of the first Easter and their public proclamation
for these developments of the record to occur. It may be
reasonable to envisage Christians a generation or two later
expressing their internal experience of Jesus as being 'like'
meeting him risen from the dead. But for the first disciples to
say it would have been to invite the response, 'But in fact he is
dead – we have seen his tomb.' Yet nobody, so far as we
know, said any such thing. The first disciples claimed that
Jesus had risen from the dead, leaving his tomb empty, and
that they had seen him. They used simple, factual language,
shorn of any notion of extravagant mystical experience.

And they were heard in that way, too, both by their friends
and their enemies. Some believed them, and were baptised.
Some rejected their claim, but not with the argument that it
was not to be taken literally. Indeed, the opposition arguments, as they have reached us down the centuries, were
feeble attempts to refute the evidence, as though they were as
baffled by the facts as the Christians were at first, but were
reluctant to draw the obvious conclusions.

There have been arguments about the historicity of the
empty tomb, but for myself I am convinced that it was a fact.
It is hard to believe that the disciples would have publicly
preached that Jesus was risen from the dead if his body were
still in the tomb, and even harder to believe that anyone
would have been converted by it if they had. Not only that,
but many scholars now believe that in the early decades of the
Church pilgrims travelled to Jerusalem to visit the tomb of
Jesus, where they recited together a narrative of the resurrection (possibly part of Mark's account).[9] Is it conceivable that
they were visiting an *occupied* tomb? That would contradict
the universally accepted belief of the early Church that the

tomb was empty – a belief which even the most radical critics recognise.

And if the tomb was empty, where was the body? We are not talking of some hole-in-the-corner affair, but of a 'Jesus Movement' which rapidly grew into a major irritation for the authorities, and had as its foundational belief the claim that Jesus had risen from the dead. These authorities had every incentive to produce the body and silence the apostles, but they were unable to do it. The clear implication is that the body could not be found, and that it could not be found because it was not where it should have been, in the tomb. The claim of the disciples to have seen the Lord, and the presence of an empty tomb, are the complementary sides of the same assertion, that Jesus who had been crucified, died and was buried was now fully alive, in the wholeness of his personality: 'body, mind and spirit', as we would say.

The resurrection is important in the total Christian revelation because it represents a divine 'seal of approval' on the life of Jesus. It is one thing to claim that God has communicated perfectly with the human race through Jesus; it is quite another to know for certain that God agrees with that claim. After all, the world has never been short of people claiming to speak or act in the name of God.

But the resurrection provides just that divine endorsement, as though God were saying, 'See, he *is* my Son. He *has* spoken in my name. I *have* accepted what he has done.' Again, it may well be a realisation of this that has led the opponents of Christianity to direct their critical fire at the resurrection. A great deal hangs on it. If it is true, then God has spoken in Jesus, and we can know it. If it is not true, or in doubt, then Christians are in no better a situation than the devotees of any other religion that claims to speak the truth of God but cannot prove it. Jesus would then take his place alongside, but not ahead of, the other great religious figures of history, and the human race would be left to speculate that God might have spoken, but we can never know for sure.

The resurrection, however, says that God has spoken, and

that we can know it. All the partial communication between the God who made us and his bewildered creatures – all the groping to understand the world around us, all the experiences of the human spirit, all the agonies of conscience and the words and images of the prophets – have found their culmination in the perfect communication of the Father through the Son.

God has spoken. He has given us 'the truth in the Son'. The only question that remains to be answered is this: 'Will we listen?'

Notes

Chapter 1

1. *The Creation*, BBC 1, March 4th, 1984, and an article in *The Listener*, March 8th, 1984
   Psalm 139:13-16
3. Genesis 1:1-13
4. Psalm 89:11-12
5. Isaiah 45:6-7
6. Revelation 4:11
7. In a talk on BBC Radio 4, March 7th, 1984, and in his book *The Way the World is* (Triangle)
8. John 1:1-5
9. Genesis 1:1-3

Chapter 2

1. *The Intelligent Universe* (Michael Joseph)
2. Psalm 139:13

Chapter 3

1. Genesis 1:27-31
2. Genesis 3:16-19
3. Genesis 3:22-24
4. Exodus 3:2-14
5. Exodus 3:7-10
6. Jeremiah 18:1-6
7. Romans 9:20-21
8. See, for example, John 8:41 and Mark 6:3

9. Luke 1:26-35
10. 1 Corinthians 15:21-22

Chapter 4

1. Hebrews 1:1-2
2. Romans 1:19-20
3. Isaiah 2:4
4. 1 Peter 1:10-12
5. Matthew 13:57
6. Luke 13:33

Chapter 5

1. *The Search for the Real Jesus* (Hodder & Stoughton)

Chapter 6

1. 2 Timothy 3:16-17
2. 2 Peter 1:21
3. 2 Peter 3:15-16
4. John 14:26
5. See Matthew 4:1-10
6. 1 Corinthians 15:3-8
7. *But This I CAN Believe* (Hodder & Stoughton)
8. *The Other Side of '84* (British Council of Churches)
9. See 1 Corinthians 2:6-16

Chapter 7

1. *The Search for the Real Jesus* (Hodder & Stoughton)
2. Geza Vermes, in *The Riddell Memorial Lectures*, 1981
3. *Jesus the Jew* (Collins)
4. *Jesus of Nazareth*
5. Mark 2:8-12

6. Matthew 22:42
7. *The Supremacy of Jesus* (Hodder & Stoughton)
8. Op. cit.
9. See, for example, *Jesus* by Edward Schillebeeckx (Collins) p 334 ff.

Bibliography

THE OTHER SIDE OF '84 by Leslie Newbiggen (British Council of Churches).

THE SUPREMACY OF JESUS by Stephen Neill (Hodder).

JESUS by Edward Schillebeeckx (Collins).

JESUS THE JEW by Geza Vermes (Collins).

THE GOSPEL OF JESUS THE JEW by Geza Vermes (University of Newcastle-upon-Tyne)

BUT THIS I CAN BELIEVE by David Winter (Hodder)

THE SEARCH FOR THE REAL JESUS by David Winter (Hodder)

THE INTELLIGENT UNIVERSE by Fred Hoyle (Michael Joseph).

FAITH IN JESUS CHRIST by John Coventry (Darton, Longman and Todd).

THE WAY THE WORLD IS by John Polkinghorne (Triangle).

THE CASE AGAINST GOD by Gerald Priestland (Collins).

THE LIVING GOD by Keith Ward (SPCK).